RIDING THE
WILD OCEAN

PAUL S. KRANTZ JR.

RIDING THE WILD OCEAN

Around Cape Cod in a Small Sloop
and Other Adventures

THE
History
PRESS

Published by The History Press
Charleston, SC
www.historypress.net

First published 2014
The History Press edition 2018

Manufactured in the United States

ISBN 9781467139021

Library of Congress Control Number: 2017963241

This content was originally published by Tate Publishing (ISBN 9781627468572).

Notice: The information in this book is true and complete to the best of our knowledge. It is offered without guarantee on the part of the author or The History Press. The author and The History Press disclaim all liability in connection with the use of this book.

ACKNOWLEDGEMENTS

First and foremost, I would like to thank my dear wife, Carol, for her tolerance, patience, and generous support of my crazy adventuring.

A sincere thank you to my daughters, Donna and Valerie, for their support and pluck in accompanying me for sails aboard the fine little yacht Yvaledon, especially after the adventure to which they were unwittingly subjected leading to the final chapter of this book.

To my dear friend, Lou LaFlamme, whose unflappable courage and unfailing companionship sustained me throughout our adventures together as told in Riding the Wild Ocean, I offer my heartfelt gratitude.

Beyond the world class artwork provided by Russ Kramer (http://www.russkramer.com/), his sage advice and editing skills contributed immensely to the final story structure and other aspects of effective presentation.

Finally, I would like to thank the entire staff at Tate Publishing for their support in making this publication possible, for allowing me an integral role in the publication process, and for the high standard of quality incorporated into the final product. I am particularly grateful to Donna Chumley, who enthusiastically accepted my initial manuscript and, by extension, inducted me into the Tate family of authors.

TABLE OF CONTENTS

CHAPTER I

BUTLER HOLE AND POLLOCK RIP

The seas continued to build, the wind now shrieking. Lou began to express concern with the narrowing channel. On the GPS screen, he could see the shoals squeezing us on both sides. Our flashing red four-second buoy was clearly visible off the port bow as we rode over wave crests but disappeared in the troughs. Once again hard on the wind, we were going to slip safely past the red flasher mid-channel. The next buoy, a flashing green about a mile to the east, was directly in our path. We had to stay to the north of that buoy to stay within the channel. Missing that to the south would take us over shallow areas of sixteen to twenty feet at the northern end of Stone Horse Shoal, the channel being generally over forty feet deep between shoals. The concern over those shallows was not bottoming out against the sandy sea floor but encountering locally larger, steeper seas. I could tack to port to reposition into the channel but preferred to avoid that risky maneuver in those dark seas if possible. Lou could feel the seas still building. He began voicing his concern that he could not control the boat in the raging maelstrom. Suddenly he cried out, "You have to take the boat. I can't control it!" Having finally regained much of my strength, I took over the tiller as it became obvious that we would miss the green flasher by a few hundred feet south of the channel. The channel turned sharply eastward around the green flashing buoy permitting us to reenter the channel if we simply maintained our current heading. In short, we would cut across the northern end of Stone Horse Shoal on a brief excursion out of the channel and reenter the channel just past the green buoy.

The time was about 4:00 a.m. Dawn would soon be breaking. We braced for our shortcut across the northern tip of Stone Horse Shoal. A foul, two-knot current gradually slid us toward the right hand side of the channel, then out of it toward the Stone Horse shallows. I monitored the depth meter: thirty-eight feet… thirty-four…thirty…twenty-nine. The seas began responding to the rising bottom as they became noticeably larger and steeper… twenty-eight feet deep…twenty-six. White water spray began raining into the cockpit. Twenty-six…thirty…forty-one feet— we were back in the channel heading across Butler Hole!

Dawn began breaking. In the dim gray light of morn, I silently went into shock at the spectacle of the seas surrounding us. Although we had been in them for hours, we had not seen the seas before that moment. I had never been in anything like that in my life. Mountains of water nearly as high as my spreader, which is halfway up my thirty-foot mast, raced by. Every wave foamed with angry, writhing energy. Spray blew from every wave top into the next trough. There was no color in that predawn world, only bleak shades of gray.

"You went into shock, and I was awestruck!" recalled Lou. "I told myself, 'wonder of wonders!' and hung on. I knew this was going to be a ride of rides, but I was truly calm through it all. I never lost faith in the captain. What a thrill! My main task at this point was to keep the cockpit as dry as I could, which was an arduous task at that."

We had been ignoring the pressure building in our bladders, not wanting to address the issue in those seas. Normally, we could have relieved ourselves over the side from a standing position either on the seats or on the deck—but not in those seas. With forces strong enough to pitch us over the side, we were forced to perform that function from a kneeling stance on a seat, firmly braced against the cockpit combing while securely grasping a lifeline stanchion in one hand and one's self in the other.

For the first time since the previous day, I could see the dinghy. At the end of its forty-foot tether, wave tops, parted by the dinghy's high-riding bow, jumped into the air in a fountain of spray briefly obliterating the dinghy from view. The little boat then dashed back into sight as it cascaded down the back side of a wave only to rise again on the next wave and repeat the performance. My comical little dinghy broke the tension as we watched its antics behind us. How it managed to stay afloat through all the action of the night, I will never know.

By 6:30 a.m., the current was going slack in Pollock Rip in preparation for flooding east. We were emerging from Butler Hole heading toward the deep waters of the open Atlantic. Monomoy Island and the Cape Cod mainland stretched northward. Chatham lay at the southeastern corner of the Cape directly north of Monomoy. Between us and calmer open water lay Pollock Rip Channel, two miles of twenty-to-thirty-foot deep water roiled with swirling currents and incoming ocean swells and whipped to a froth by the stiff north wind. On either side lay deadly, unseen reefs and the scattered remains of dozens of hapless boats and ships. As the slack current began to flood, carrying us with it, the moving water heading east from Nantucket Sound into Butler Hole and Pollock Rip turned north in and around Pollock Rip to run parallel to the coastline. There, in Pollock Rip, where the incoming ocean swells meet the turning, swirling tidal currents, strange things happen.

The incoming swells were entering Pollock Rip, generally from the east, at different speeds and from slightly different directions due to the drag of the uneven and shallow bottom contours. This resulted in colliding mountains of water. Where crests invaded troughs, relatively flat seas ensued. Where merging crests and troughs coincided, huge rogue waves formed with spectacular results. Superimposed on this were the twisting, churning current and the unrelenting north wind. For us, the current became a mixed blessing. While sweeping us forward in the general direction of our intended route, the current was running against the incoming ocean swells causing them to steepen and topple. Rip seas of this nature are normally formed by tidal currents and wind running in opposing directions, causing the wind driven seas to steepen and topple. In Pollock Rip, the wind from the north set up its own wave pattern of ten-to-twelve-foot seas, which ran at right angles to the heavier ocean swells entering from the east against the current from the west. Into this mad turmoil we plunged on a magnetic (compass) heading of sixty degrees.

At least it was daylight. We could see the enemy.

Again, Lou recounted his impressions: "All I perceived at this time was a sea with an incomparable rage not truly understanding the forces in motion to cause it, and I wasn't about to ask questions of the captain then."

The sudden change in depth from forty-plus feet of water in Butler Hole to less than thirty feet in Pollock Rip was immediately felt. Seas began striking the boat at odd angles sending water into the cockpit and over our heads into the sail. My first instinct was to try and find a way to contact each wave in a manner that would minimize the water taken into the cockpit. But that had to be done without too much sacrifice to our heading and ground track. The rogue waves were the worst. They seemed to travel in pairs and caused us to lose ground, but the rogues were usually followed by relatively flat seas where we could recover the lost ground. As I began to recognize wave forms that would slam into the bow and dump heavy amounts of water into the cockpit, I became somewhat adept at swinging the bow away just enough to soften the blow and allow most of the collapsing wave top to slide under the hull rather than crashing against it. I could not spot or react in time to them all, and for that, I was always punished. Actually, Lou was punished; he did the bailing!

So intent was I on dancing with the waves, I never saw it coming. Seemingly out of nowhere, a solid green sea, moving upwind, came over the low (starboard) rail at shoulder height and marched right into the cockpit, dumping the greatest amount of water we had taken aboard so far. Where the hell did that come from? Meanwhile, the steep swells kept coming at the bow. Now I had to keep an eye to starboard as well as forward. We could not take another one of those. As the huge ocean swells collided, they occasionally squeezed out secondary waves, like peas from a pod, sending them upwind until they spent themselves in a futile drive against all the forces working against them. We just happened to get caught in the path of one of those secondaries. I saw the next one and modified my dance accordingly, swinging the stern away from the sea allowing the invading wave to slide sweetly under the hull. On and on we danced. Two miles never seemed so far! But the roughest ride was still ahead.

The end was in sight: a huge red gong buoy marking the pinch point of Pollock Rip Channel and its exit to the clear, deep, open Atlantic. Around the buoy lay water between ten and thirty feet deep, the deepest path being through about twenty-six feet of water around the south side. Our course around the south side of the buoy would take us over one or more submerged wrecks not visible from the surface but identified on the chart. Fourteen-foot seas would reduce the water depth in the wave troughs from twenty-six to nineteen feet, each wave being half above and half below the nominal surface level. Water depth in Pollock Rip had been averaging roughly twenty-six to thirty feet. I glanced at the depth meter and compass whenever I could take my eyes, just for an instant, off the attacking waves.

Twenty-three feet deep…twenty-two…twenty-one… now every foot lost in depth made a huge increase in wave height and steepness. *Yvaledon* soldiered ahead. Lou bailed for his life! The bailing, he later mused, "was continuous and feverish. But I was truly calm throughout, just busy." Twenty feet…nineteen…Seas crashed against the bow lifting it to an alarming angle and then swept over the cabin and dodger into the reefed main dragging the boat over onto its side and spilling out of the sail back into the ocean. Dear God, when will this end?

The oncoming seas, having risen to at least fifteen feet in height, were traveling so fast and were so steep that as the boat lifted to rise to each occasion, the buoyancy accelerated the boat upward pressing me down into my seat with a force that made my 150-pound frame feel more like two hundred pounds. At the top of each wave, the wind would strike the sail with its full force, after having been somewhat sheltered in the previous trough. The boat would lay over and plunge into the next trough while shedding hundreds of pounds of water. Those rip seas were so much more terrifying than simple wind driven seas of the same height! The confused rip seas lacked the symmetry of ordinary wind waves. As a result, the boat would be slammed unexpectedly by the huge waves, violently jolting our bodies in random directions for which we were never fully prepared or properly braced. I struggled to control my panic, fighting an urge to jump over the side to get away from the violence and noise and terror aboard the boat. Somehow, the distant sea several hundred feet away seemed calmer, quieter—even safer—than the madness in our wretched boat.

But why, oh why was I even out here in this little boat? And, what in God's name ever possessed me to take an old man with me in such horrendous conditions in so dangerous a stretch of wilderness? Surely, I should be committed, having taken total leave of my senses! My gradual, swirling slide into this eye of madness began a long time ago.

"Yvaledon in Pollock Rip"

CHAPTER II

A LONG TIME AGO

Riding the wild ocean in search of adventure is a pursuit that I developed during my teens in the 1950s while sailing my father's boats out of Harwichport along the southern coast of Cape Cod. During my early teens, we had a thirteen-foot Whitecap sailboat built by the Oldtown Canoe Co. in Oldtown, Maine. This was a lapstrake (overlapping) cedar planked craft with thin, wide, closely spaced oak ribs like a canoe. The result was a lightweight, sturdy, agile, and well-balanced centerboard sloop. She was a pretty little boat with a varnished interior, white exterior, and a varnished mahogany deck and transom.

During our summer vacations in Harwichport, the Whitecap was kept on a mooring in Allen Harbor where my brother, Laurence, and I had constant access to the boat. The route from the harbor entrance to a large whistle buoy two miles offshore passed over a small reef. The shallow water over the reef would cause the seas to increase in height and steepness. What fun that was! We sailed back and forth over that reef so many times I was afraid we would wear it away. We always looked forward to a day that was windier than any we had sailed in before. Eventually, windier days became harder to come by. Then, one day the wind blew at thirty-five knots as measured at the marina. Both the wind and the current were coming in toward shore. This was perfect because if I lost control and capsized the boat, it and we would simply wash ashore presumably unharmed. Teenage logic is wonderful. With the wind shrieking, Laurence and I ran to the harbor, jumped into the dinghy, rowed out to the boat, put on our life jackets, reefed the main, set sail, and headed out. No need to ask permission to use the boat today. Dad always said yes, and time was wasting.

Seas were running about four feet high, and the boat felt like it was made of tinfoil in that wind. A veil of spray swept from wave to wave as each one broke and surrendered its foamy top to the wind. We were immediately soaked by flying water as we emerged from the shelter of the breakwater at the harbor entrance. At close range the seas over the reef looked larger than they did from afar, but they still looked doable, so in we went on a close reach. The first reef wave upended the boat so abruptly that Laurence and I fell backward grasping for anything we could hold on to. The jib caught a gust and instantly ripped to shreds, allowing the boat to turn directly into the wind and seas. The second wave washed us back into deeper and somewhat calmer water. Now with the cockpit sloshing with water making the boat even more unstable, and a torn jib, two very frightened young lads tucked the tiller between their legs and retreated to the safety and comfort of Allen Harbor. This was followed by a long walk home to face Dad. Several lessons were learned that day.

Having pretty much OD'd on high winds and seas, the next reasonable challenge was night sailing. With only a flashlight, we began venturing out at sundown and beyond, past the edge of darkness. Moonlit nights gave us a little extra dark time. I was rudely awakened one morning at about 1:00 a.m. by my best friend, Howie Nicholson, who was staying with us for the week. The moon was full, a warm breeze was blowing, and teen excitement was spilling over. We ran to the harbor and sailed for two hours in the moonlight. Night sailing was a blast! Still, distant ports beckoned.

Hyannis and back, about fourteen miles, looked like a one-day sail. Dad's Mobil road map of the Cape showed several shoreline landmarks and offshore buoys including our whistle buoy. We had a chart! And I had my Boy Scout compass. We were ready!

I did notice that my compass seemed to be pointing in the wrong direction. One end of the needle, with a little copper wire wrapped around it, pointed south instead of north. Obviously, that little wire was placed there to indicate north, otherwise the needle would be perfectly symmetrical and there would be no way to tell north from south. In my blissful ignorance, I had no clue that the little copper wire was placed on the south-seeking end of the needle as a counterbalance weight to force the needle to sit level, parallel to the earth's surface. Without that weight, the symmetrical needle would point at a downward angle into the earth directly at *magnetic north*, which is near the North Pole (*true north*) and several hundred miles below the earth's surface within the earth's molten core. This molten magnet drifts slowly beneath the earth's crust such that magnetic north migrates westward away from true north at the rate of about several minutes (One minute = one-sixtieth degree) annually. As a result of the magnetic drift within the earth's core, the thirteen-degree-westward *variation* that existed when I made my first sail to Hyannis in 1954 is almost fifteen degrees today.[1]

The variation of magnetic north from true north also changes significantly as one sails great distances around the globe due to the changing geometry between magnetic and true north. For this reason, long distance sailors generally prefer to navigate using true compass directions rather than magnetic. Also, sextant sightings to the stars, sun, and other planets are referenced to a grid of latitude and longitude based on true north that aligns with

---

[1] The chaotic migratory track of magnetic north over the past four hundred years can be found in Appendix A. Note that during the past one hundred years, the track has been consistently north-northwest and is currently moving at a rate of approximately fifty-five kilometers (thirty-four miles) per year.

the overall geometry of our solar system. So with none of this cumbersome knowledge muddling our young brains, Laurence and I set out for Hyannis with a lunch Mom prepared for us, my trusty but "backward" compass, and our "chart."

We selected a clear, sunny day with gentle southwest winds. That wind direction assured us of a speedy return from Hyannis on a broad reach with the wind behind us, once we decided to return home. The sail to Hyannis would take longer, as we would be on a close reach, with the wind coming from a frontal angle. The one-to-two-foot seas that day bounced the boat around enough to set the compass needle spinning wildly in complete circles. A Boy Scout compass has no motion damping because there is no need for that in the woods where the ground is absolutely still. By holding the compass in my hand, enough stability was achieved to get a general heading, and that was good enough. So on we went. The "chart" showed a windmill in Dennisport, next to Harwichport, and by gosh, we saw it from the boat. We knew where we were! A lighthouse was also depicted on the "chart." We saw that too as we sailed a little farther along the coast. We knew when we had reached Hyannis because we recognized the port, having been there many times by car and by ferry, and we found the buoy that was on our "chart." This process of comparing actual landmarks, buoys, etc., with their respective symbols on a chart to determine one's location is a navigational technique known as piloting. The use of a compass to determine direction of travel, as well as location, is called dead reckoning. We were using both techniques in a rudimentary fashion to track our progress to and from Hyannis that day.

The sail back was longer than I had anticipated, and the day was drawing well into afternoon. I began to worry about running out of daylight. At long last, with the reddening sun beginning to warm the horizon, we could see familiar coastline and knew we were approaching Allen Harbor. From a few hundred yards offshore, we could see a lady in a skirt waving to us. It was Mom!

We waved back excitedly. We did not see the tears of relief and joy streaming down her face washing away the previous tears of dread and fear that her two sons had been lost at sea perhaps never to be seen again. Rounding the breakwater into Allen Harbor, we moored the boat and headed home. As we all converged on the little cottage on Ginger Plum Lane, Mom had arrived first and busied herself preparing a late-evening meal. We burst in blurting out our tales of adventure on the high seas. Mom carefully concealed her distress, reluctant to dampen our elation over our mighty conquest of the sea. Dad suppressed his anger and held his counsel for the same reason while at the same time swelling with pride at our success. During the following days, my parents gently but firmly made us aware of the anxiety to which we had subjected them by our late day return home from Hyannis. Had we been more considerate, we might have turned around earlier in the day to arrive back home at a more reasonable hour. Again, under the wise and patient guidance of our loving parents, we advanced a few more steps along the path to adulthood.

Such was my introduction to adventure sailing. Years went by and my sailing experience continued to grow. By the age of nineteen, I was living and working on a forty-one-foot ketch, *Rosa II*, out of City Island, New York. Lester Rosenblatt, a renowned naval architect, owned the *Rosa II*. Mr. Rosenblatt employed me for three summers during my college years at Worcester Tech. During those summers, I received intense training from him in sailboat racing, seamanship, navigation, proper yachting etiquette and history, and the basics of naval architecture. We worked closely with Mr. Richard Valentine, Mr. Rosenblatt's sailmaker. By the end of my tenure, I could look at a hull form and sail plan and know generally how that boat would behave under sail and in a seaway.

Having learned great respect from Mr. Rosenblatt for the Wizard of Bristol, Nathaniel Herreshoff, foremost designer of

America's Cup defenders of the early twentieth century, I knew that my first boat would be one of Mr. Herreshoff's small boat designs. Cape Cod Shipbuilding, currently the oldest boatyard in the country and still operating after over one hundred years in business, has the exclusive rights to building Herreshoff designs. I selected the sixteen-foot Bull's Eye sloop, a single mast sailboat with a large mainsail and a small forward jib, and only a twelve-and-a-half-foot waterline, for my first boat. I was not disappointed. Cape Cod Shipbuilding builds a high quality boat worthy of the Herreshoff design.

My first multiday, long-distance sails in open water were made in the Bull's Eye. My first venture around the Cape was also made in the Bull's Eye in 1975. At that time there were no GPS systems, and no calculators, at least none that I could afford. I navigated with paper charts, tidal current charts, an Eldridge Tide and Pilot book, a compass, dividers, protractor, a hand-bearing compass, and a six-inch slide rule for making calculations. The boat had no engine, so I learned how to anchor under sail and how to approach a dock safely under sail, which can be done with any combination of wind and current. Many of the sailing and seamanship skills learned or developed in the Bull's Eye became important backups for the adventures aboard my current boat, *Yvaledon*. The adventures in both boats, as they were sailed around Cape Cod thirty-three years apart, will unfold for the reader in the following pages. The contrast between available technologies in the 1970s and today, and the resulting impact on sailing techniques, make for additional fun and instructive reading.

CHAPTER III

POLLOCK RIP AND CHATHAM BAR REMEMBERED

My long time sailing companion, Roy Debski and I feverishly gathered our things in a small rented room that we shared on the second floor of a private residence close to the docks in Nantucket. The house was nestled under one of dozens of huge American elms planted by the early settlers along all the central streets in town. Sufficiently isolated miles offshore, Nantucket's elms were never struck by Dutch elm disease. In the lengthening shadows of a sunny August afternoon, we carried our boat bags, a fresh supply of ice, and sandwiches to our waiting dinghy and rowed out to the Bull's Eye gently tugging at its anchor close to shore.

Very little conversation transpired between us as Roy and I became increasingly anxious about the unknown but certain dangers that lay ahead. At least the weather was favorable, even perfect, with a warm and gentle breeze from the southwest, which would stay with us for the next several days. We knew the drill. Roy boarded the boat and took the bags. I boarded the boat and secured the dinghy to an aft cleat leaving a short length of line between the two boats to minimize our total profile in the crowded harbor. I then securely stowed our cargo in the cuddy cabin (crawl space) under the foredeck and closed the door to the bulkhead sealing off our belongings from the weather. I pulled in some anchor line to shorten the scope and minimize the amount of line we would have to deal with under sail. Meanwhile, Roy fed the mainsail into the slot in the boom and secured the tack to the gooseneck fitting (that attaches the boom to the mast) at the forward end with a pin made specifically for that purpose. He then pulled the foot of the sail taught with the clew outhaul at the aft end and made that short length of line fast on a small cleat at the aft end of the boom. He next attached the halyard to the head of the sail and began to haul down on the halyard while at the same time feeding the sail into the slot in the mast. Still without a word to each other, Roy continued to raise the main taking care not to let it fill and drive us forward on the anchor. I went aft to tend the tiller and to keep the mainsheet from catching on the tiller, which would allow the luffing sail to fill prematurely. Roy raised the jib and began slowly pulling in the anchor line, pausing just before allowing the anchor to break free to let the boat swing into position for an initial port tack. When I said, "Okay," he broke the anchor free. As I felt the anchor release its hold on the bottom, I carefully pulled in the sails easing us forward and under way. At this particularly critical moment, when the anchor breaks free, one must be alert for initial reverse movement, or backing of the boat, should the sails not immediately fill, in which case the tiller must be reversed (pushed to starboard) to prevent falling onto the opposite (starboard) tack. As soon as the sails fill and backward motion stops, the tiller must be reversed again in preparation for forward movement to maintain the port tack. While I adjusted the sheets and the boat's heading for as little forward speed as possible, Roy sloshed the anchor up and down to clean off the sediment prior to pulling the anchor, chain, and remaining line into the cockpit and securing them under the port seat. I could now turn the boat north and head for Pollock Rip.

With the wind at our backs and a calm sea, our confidence returned along with the excitement and anticipation of great adventure. The plan was to sail through the night in the wide open but protected waters of Nantucket Sound so that we would arrive at the narrowing entrance to Butler Hole and Pollock Rip

Channel in daylight with plenty of time to search for the entrance to Chatham Harbor in the afternoon. A quick look at most any map reveals an open expanse of water from Nantucket Sound eastward to the open Atlantic. However, a closer inspection of chart details further reveals a continuous shallow reef, easily a hundred square miles in area, extending from Nantucket Island northward to the southern tip of Monomoy Island. Monomoy juts southward from Chatham on the southeastern tip of Cape Cod for a distance of approximately seven miles and is the only visible division, other than Nantucket Island itself, between Nantucket Sound and the open ocean to the east. Yet for all that open water, the only navigable deep water is through Butler Hole and Pollock Rip Channel at Monomoy's southern tip or through Great Round Shoal Channel just north of Nantucket heading, for us, in the wrong direction. Pollock Rip is a natural, undredged waterway through which the surging tidal currents flow with intense vigor. More will be described of this extraordinary channel, quite possibly one of the most difficult and dangerous anywhere along the eastern seaboard. Pollock Rip is a black diamond run, not anyplace for the novice sailor or anyone else lacking extensive open water experience.

As Nantucket dropped farther astern, the seas built gradually with the lengthening fetch. Dense marine traffic in and out of Nantucket Harbor comprising yachts of all sizes, commercial boats, and ferries all disappeared to the west heading to or from other civilized ports of call such as Hyannis, Martha's Vineyard, Newport, and the like. We alone headed north. The vast shoals to the east protected us from incoming ocean swells. This was the time to eat. There would be no time for that later. A sandwich, water, coke, an apple, and we were done.

The next task was to confirm our heading and position on the chart, carefully protected in a large watertight clear vinyl envelope. The envelope also gave the paper chart some heft to prevent the wind from too easily casting it overboard. Spare charts and another envelope were in the cuddy. Currents in Nantucket Sound generally run east and west with local variations dependent on the bottom contours and land outcroppings. On an hourly basis, new headings were calculated using the Eldridge Tide and Pilot Book and associated tidal current charts. The Eldridge gave us the exact time of day the current went slack (turning either east or west) each day at Pollock Rip Channel. The tidal current charts gave us the exact current velocities (speed and direction) everywhere in Nantucket Sound and surrounding waters using dozens of tiny numbered arrows spread all over each page. Each of the twelve pages represents one or more hours past slack current at Pollock Rip. The first six pages show the flooding cycle at one-hour intervals, the first page being labeled "flood starts" (current turns east)[1]. The "flood starts" page is one of two pages that shows the tidal current velocities in the Nantucket Sound area when the current is slack in Pollock Rip Channel. The next page is "one hour after flood starts," etc. The last six pages represent the ebbing cycle at one-hour intervals. The "ebb starts" (current turns west) page is the other page showing the current velocities in the area when the current is slack in Pollock Rip Channel. The last page is labeled "five hours after ebb starts." Using this information, along with an estimate of our boat's average speed through the water, the time of day, and our known position on the chart, we could calculate the angle needed either to the left or right of our desired course in order to counteract the current at our position, at that time of day, and on that date in order to maintain course toward our intended destination. Since the tide cycle is slightly longer than twelve hours, the times of slack current at any given location (Pollock Rip in our case) change from day to day.

The most difficult values to estimate or determine accurately are the boat's average speed through the water and, most problematic of all, the average speed and direction of current for the next hour. Through experience, the boat's speed can be fairly reliably estimated to within a few tenths of a knot. The current is another matter. In a small boat such as the Bull's Eye, with an average speed typically from one to five knots, the effect of crosscurrents of up to three knots can result in major heading corrections to maintain course. Sizeable errors can be catastrophic, especially in the fog or at night, and even in broad daylight in a place like Pollock Rip. Every effort was made to accurately estimate the local current speed and direction. That included correcting the speed values on the current charts for major influences such as the moon's phase (new, half, or full), position in its elliptical orbit (apogee or perigee), and declination (position either north or south of the earth's equator). Moon phase and position in its orbit can alter current speeds by as much as 50 percent, so I always made a correction for the moon's influence as advised in Eldridge.

The actual calculations for determining the correcting angle to counteract tidal current effects were done geometrically by drawing lines on the paper charts with a pencil. For example, for a 1.5 knot current, a 1.5-inch line (tidal current vector) would be drawn in the direction of flow, as shown on the tidal current chart, from the boat's position on the navigational (NOAA) chart. At the end of that tidal current vector, one arm of the dividers would be placed. The second arm would be opened to a distance in inches equal to the estimated speed of the boat, let's say three knots. The dividers would then be swung in a three-inch arc until the second arm touched the course line. That point was marked. A pencil line was then drawn from the end of the tidal current vector to that new point on the course line thus completing a "current triangle." The angle between that last line drawn and the course line gave us the angular correction for our new heading. In fact, the angle between that last line drawn and magnetic north was our new heading and could be measured directly on the chart. We can call that last line drawn the "new heading line." The distance, in inches, from the boat's position on the chart to where the new heading line intersected the course line gave us our expected speed made good over the ground. Got all that? Multiplication and division calculations to determine such things as our estimated time of arrival at the next mark were performed using a six-inch-long aluminum slide rule since affordable calculators had not hit the market yet in the early 1970s. The above three paragraphs look like a challenging hour exam for an advanced high school math class. Such heading corrections were routinely completed at least once every hour that we were under way in less than ten minutes, day and night, regardless of weather or sea conditions. Unexpected weather changes demanded additional corrections.

In between heading corrections, efforts were made to confirm actual position since our fancy calculations were sometimes completely out to lunch. With a horizon limit of only about four miles sitting and no more than seven miles standing on deck, much time was spent out of sight of land. All sightings were, therefore, to be valued as navigational opportunities.

Knowing our exact position was not as important as knowing that we were on course. Several techniques are available to determine that. For example, let's assume that the course from buoy A to target buoy B is 0 degrees (due north). As you leave buoy A behind, it should remain on a back azimuth of 180 degrees. However, if a tidal current is flowing from west to east and you have made no correction, your back azimuth will increase to 181, 182, 183, etc., as you drift with the current off course to the right. In order to correct for the drift of the current, you will need to steer to the left. You will have to oversteer to get back on course then adjust as necessary to maintain course. If you had made a calculation (with a current triangle) for the effect of the current using Eldridge and the tidal current charts, and your calculation is correct, your back azimuth to buoy A would remain steady at 180 degrees without further correction. A hand bearing compass is most useful for determining the exact bearing (such as the back azimuth to buoy A) of a buoy or any other mark. We used a device commonly referred to as a "hockey puck" because of its shape, color, and size. This hand bearing compass imposes the compass image directly on the target being measured, so there is never any question about coordinating the timing of the reading to coincide with lining up the target as there is with many other hand bearing compass designs.

The same determination of heading correction can be made using target buoy B, if buoy B is in sight. If you are drifting to the right with the current, buoy B will go from 0 degrees to 359, 358, etc. A corrected course to the left will have to be made in the same manner as when using a back azimuth from buoy A as a reference. Other techniques for determining position will be discussed later on.

People often ask, "What do you do on a sailboat all day long?" I usually stammer out some nonsense not knowing where to begin.

As night fell, Great Point on the northern tip of Nantucket was visible to the east and a flashing green buoy was several miles dead ahead, as it should have been. We were on course. All target buoys from this point on were lighted. The next buoy, six and a half miles beyond the flashing green at the entrance to Butler Hole was a flashing red near the southern tip of Monomoy Island. A land based beacon on Monomoy Point flashed white at ten-second intervals. The weather was clear, but the current was increasingly against us as we had to turn toward the northeast from the flashing green toward the flashing red at Butler Hole. With a steady five to ten-knot breeze with us, we made reasonable progress. Yet arrival at Butler Hole would not be much before sunrise as planned. Given our rate of progress over the ground against the current in the light air, we could anticipate spending most of the night covering the ten miles to Butler Hole.

Preparations were made for darkness. Navigating tools, charts, and flashlights were assembled on the starboard seat where they could be found easily. We were on a port tack with the wind off the port quarter, so the starboard seat was on the low side where things would be less inclined to roll off onto the floor. The dinghy was towing easily at the end of a forty-foot tether. Navigation lights were turned on. All was well.

Staying on course as we approached the flashing red buoy off Monomoy was crucial. The deep, wide waters of Nantucket Sound narrow as in a funnel toward Butler Hole. On either side are shallows that rise above the surface in some spots and frequently offer only one or two feet of water in others at low water. These deadly areas are named Handkerchief Shoals to the west and Stone Horse Shoals to the east. Heading into the most desolate area around Cape Cod, miles from any inhabited land, darkness was almost total. Usually, some reflected light from nearby towns softens the darkness. Not here. Monomoy Island harbors not a soul. The horizon was invisible, except that I knew it was somewhere near where the stars ended. A moon would have helped immensely, but that was not to be that night. Only a cloudy night blacking out the stars would have been worse. With an increasing loss of one's sense of up and down, and straight ahead, as the boat bounces around in the seaway of a black night, vertigo becomes a potential danger depriving one of the ability to focus the eyes to read a chart or to take a bearing, not to mention inducing motion sickness. Watching the lighted compass card can help to avert or, if necessary, relieve vertigo. If only a single star is visible, looking at that also helps. Staying alert from minute to minute as the nighttime hours slowly grind by, watching the compass readings swing around as the boat yaws left and right and trying to keep the boat's average heading centered on the correct value is a fatiguing task. This continuum is punctuated only by the need to take hand bearing compass readings to confirm course and position. The cool dampness of the night eventually penetrates clothing to bring on a lasting chill adding to the fatigue of continually bracing against the constant motion of the boat. Add to this an increasing need of sleep and the night can seem long indeed. Upon approaching Butler Hole, the gentle swells from the open sea began to make themselves felt as they traveled largely unfettered through Pollock Rip Channel and Butler Hole.

Several large lighted buoys marked the path through Butler Hole and Pollock Rip Channel at approximately one-to-two-mile intervals. The buoy lights can be seen at a greater distance at night than can the buoys themselves in the daytime. Staying in the channel is paramount. The currents are swift and can sweep a craft out of the channel and into the shallows in an instant. In light winds, the possibility of the two-plus knot current exceeding my boat's speed was not out of the question. The light wind held steady and kept us moving forward. The current was against us entering Butler Hole but turned with us as flood began, and we progressed eastward through Pollock Rip into the rising sun. Had the wind died while we were in that channel, we could have conceivably been forced to deploy the anchor to keep from being swept into the shallows and dashed to pieces in the shallow water of deep wave troughs, or as an alternative, we could have allowed the current to sweep us back from whence we came as long as we had enough air in the sails to maneuver ourselves to stay within the channel. Such desperate options were not to be, but survival options must always be considered ahead of time for the same reason that life jackets are always carried aboard. Contingency plans and safety equipment go hand in hand.

One must travel at least four miles east past Monomoy Island to clear Bearse Shoal to the north before heading north toward Chatham. The entire area is littered with wrecked ships and boats, most of which are not visible above the surface, but which offer additional navigational interest as they reach upward to snag the unwary seaman.

One such wreck was of particular interest to me. The wreck of the tanker, *Pendleton*, on the eastern end of Bearse Shoal, lay on its side in fifteen to twenty feet of water and was almost directly in my path to Chatham. I had never seen such a large wreck at close range, and this was my opportunity. We headed directly for it.

Our passage to this point had been so smooth that I failed to beware of the sudden dangers that can erupt without warning and that make this area so notorious to mariners. Sailing along in gentle five- or six-foot-high ocean swells, the horizon unexpectedly disappeared in all directions. We found ourselves careening down the inside of a huge bowl shaped trough as if swallowed into a sinkhole. At the bottom of this watery bowl I could see the sandy ocean floor reflecting the bright sunlight. Were we going to slam down onto the sand? As we slid across the bottom of the bowl, the eastern side of it began to cave in toward us in the form of a huge bulge that quickly filled the bowl without creating any foam or white water. This was a terrifying sight as the upper edge of the collapsing bowl was at least three or four feet above our heads. Somehow the boat lifted as if being wedged upward by the invading bulge of green water and wound up on the surface where we could once again see all around us. The deck remained completely dry throughout this entire mad excursion.

The ocean had turned into a pocked, watery moonscape. Everywhere we looked we could see standing bowl-shaped troughs forming and disappearing, but otherwise not moving along the surface in any direction. Incredibly, I had not noticed our approach into this strange sea form. Such phenomenon is the result of a confluence of tidal currents and incoming ocean swells. To understand how such odd wave patterns can develop, one must first look at how incoming ocean swells are affected by decreasing water depth as the sea floor rises ultimately to the beach. The energy of ocean swells runs deep like rolling, watery icebergs. As the swells begin to feel the drag of the rising sea bottom, they gradually slow their advance toward shore. This in turn steepens the swells as their momentum continues to carry them forward. The shallower the water becomes, the greater the drag on the swells and the slower they advance toward the beach. This deceleration below the surface steepens the waves above the surface until they begin to topple **forming typical surfing waves or** combers. Combers are formed from Chatham to Provincetown, fifty miles to the north, in a continuous array between one-half to three-quarters of a mile wide along the entire length of unbroken beach. Beyond Chatham there is no safe haven before Provincetown. When the sea floor is hilly, or otherwise uneven, as in the Monomoy-Chatham vicinity, the swells turn and change direction as one end is slowed more than the other. This tends to cause the swells to move at different speeds and in different directions and eventually to collide with one another. Wave crests moving over wave troughs cancel each other out forming areas of flat or smaller seas. On the other hand, crests moving over crests (and troughs into troughs) create larger than normal, or rogue, waves. When all of this activity moves into a region of opposing or swirling tidal currents, the wave motion can be brought to a near standstill creating standing waves, or in our case, the strange, standing, bowl-shaped wave troughs. These odd trough formations were occurring a few miles offshore well before the start of the comber field. We sailed into several more bowl-shaped troughs before exiting into a more conventional seaway.

As we approached closer to the *Pendleton*, my fascination grew. The rusting hulk loomed ever larger as details of that sentinel of death came increasingly into focus in the bright midday sun. Whatever became of the terrified crew as their ship broke apart in horrific seas on Bearse Shoal. Where was the front half of the ship? Only the stern half remained on the reef. The huge propeller and rudder were half in and half out of the water. Her barnacled bottom faced us. Most of the bottom paint was gone, and judging from the advanced state of rust, the ship had been there for quite a while.

> According to Mr. Peter L. Reagan of the Metro West Dive Club, on Tuesday, February 12, 1952, the 1944 vintage 10,448 ton, 504 foot long welded steel T-2 tanker *Pendleton* departed Baton Rouge, Louisiana on a five day voyage to Boston with a cargo of number 2 fuel oil. She

encountered a severe storm off Cape Hatteras, North Carolina that stayed with her. She continued up the coast at half speed. By Monday morning, February 18, 1952, about 5 miles east of Chatham, disaster struck. She split in two. There was no time to send an SOS. While headed back to Chatham after assisting with the rescue of yet another T-2 tanker, the *Fort Mercer*, that also split in half in the same storm about 6 hours before the *Pendleton*, a Coast Guard pilot saw half a ship rolling in the surf off Chatham. Flying lower, he made out the name…*Pendleton!*

The Massachusetts Office of Coastal Zone Management offers further details of the Pendleton disaster:

An east-northeasterly gale was blowing, attended by heavy snow and seas 60 to 70 feet in height. Two large waves hit the vessel. Following a "loud explosive sound," the tanker broke in two trapping 8 men on the bow and 33 in the stern. The radio room was in the bow and the electrical generator in the stern, thus neither set of crew could dispatch an SOS.

Eventually alerted by radar, a 36-foot Coast Guard motor lifeboat, under the command of Bernard C. Webber departed the Chatham Lifeboat Station just before 6:00 PM. Everything was fine until they hit Chatham Bar where the situation turned critical. "When we hit the bar I thought we smashed up," said Webber. The other men were knocked to the deck time after time. I thought several times I had lost my whole crew. They looked like goners but they managed to hold on."

By little more than instinct, his compass having gone overboard crossing the bar, Webber navigated his lifeboat through 40-foot seas up to the *Pendleton's* stern. Considered an extraordinary feat of seamanship in such conditions, the mission has gone down as one of the most heroic rescues in the annals of the United States Coast Guard.

Thirty-two of the thirty-three tanker's stern survivors were rescued. Only the ship's cook, Ordinary Seaman, George C. Meyers perished.

Red flares dropped from circling aircraft illuminated the scene like a watery battle zone. A rope Jacob's ladder was hung down the starboard side of the stern. The crew climbed down the ladder but had to jump the last few feet as the next-to-bottom rung was missing. Meyers helped hand down half of his shipmates to the waiting Coast Guard lifeboat before the last three, including him, were forced to jump. He got on the lifeboat, but fell off as a wave caught the craft. Several men tried to pull Meyers aboard, but were unsuccessful due to his 350 pound weight and the violent tossing of the boat. Soon thereafter, another wave caught the lifeboat and crushed Meyers against the tanker's hull.

Pendleton's stern continued to drift southward before grounding off Monomoy. There were no survivors from the tanker's bow. One by one, mountainous seas swept them from the vessel as rescuers watched helplessly, unable to work in close due to shallow waters and high seas. *Pendleton's* bow ran aground on Pollock Rip Shoal and was eventually swept away. Only the stern half remained as a grim reminder of that fateful voyage.

I wanted to sail around to the other side of *Pendleton's* stern to peer into the broken middle and to see the deck visible only from the west side. Again I dropped my guard as I stared in awe at the spectacle that now lay within a few hundred feet of us. The sea was not finished toying with us and our little boat.

As we rounded the north end of the wreck, I tried to see into the broken middle, but darkness within the hull and internal bulkheads blocked the view. Ripped and twisted hull plates, where the vessel broke apart, surrounding the dark interior looked like the maw of a great shark. The seas breaking against the hulk gave it an aura of immobility like that of a permanent rock outcropping. I cannot imagine the savagery of the seas that could sweep such a monolith off its base like a bird off its perch. The deck was now coming into view on the west side. The rusty deck plates, cleats, and other deck hardware still in place were streaked with years of accumulated guano from seagulls, cormorants, and other sea birds. The black, single, round engine exhaust stack stuck out of the deck just forward of the fantail at an almost horizontal angle but perpendicular to the near vertical deck. As I recall, a cable guy may have been supporting it.

Wham! Suddenly we were nearly horizontal on our beam ends, water pouring over the side into the cockpit. An outrageous wind came out of nowhere knocking us down and swinging us around onto the starboard tack. Struggling to recover the lost mainsheet that had dropped from my grasp, I could see it unreaving through its blocks until a stopper knot at the bitter end prevented it from totally unrigging itself. If I could only get her into the wind to swing the boom over center, I could grab the sheet, pull it back in, and reset the main. This I did. In all the confusion I had barely noticed that the wind had returned to its former gentle self. What was going on, and where did that wind come from?

As we regained our composure and control of the boat, Roy bailed out the cockpit, and I prepared to resume our excursion around the *Pendleton*. We could see no trace of extraordinary wind on the water in the form of typical cat's paws, so we gingerly ventured forth, once again, around the west side of the wreck.

Wham! Again, we were on our beam ends in the grip of this invisible wind. And again, we were wheeled around onto the starboard tack and shoved into the calm air at the north end of the wreck. This time I had managed to hang onto the mainsheet and maintain control of the boat. Were we in some kind of twilight zone? How were we going to get into Chatham?

With minds in high gear, we gradually came to the realization that the hot midday sun was baking the sands of Monomoy which, in turn, heated and expanded the south-to-southwest breeze, accelerating the air over the hot sands to create the invisible "wind tunnel" into which we had sailed. That local band of high-speed air extended for several miles before dissipating. The hot wind accelerating off the Monomoy sands never dropped to the level of the water to roil its surface and disclose its presence. Armed with this new awareness, we snuck along the western edge of the wreck out of reach of the hot wind and completed a circle around the broken hull. As we did so, we could hear the seas breaking against the east side of the ship with an eerie echo resounding within the hull.

With our curiosity satisfied by a sail-around of the wreck, we now had to find a break in the surf where we could enter Chatham before nightfall. We knew that the fishing fleet would soon arrive to reach the Chatham fish pier before six o'clock. After that, their entire boatloads of fish would drop to half price because it would be too late to distribute the catch to local restaurants and retail outlets for sale that day. An after-six catch would instantly become one day old and be worth only half the fresh fish price. This was a major incentive to reach the fish pier before the 6:00 p.m. witching hour, inspiring even desperate efforts to succeed. The tide was low at about 4:30 p.m. making crossing the bar especially challenging. However, the fishing boat captains would surely know how to do it, so we could follow them in. Our boat drew only two and a half feet; the fishing boats drew at least four feet fully loaded with fish. Our NOAA chart gave no details of the area, offering only a cryptic note that bottom contours are subject to change due to continually shifting sands and to enter only with local knowledge.[2]

---

[2] To better assist the reader in following the path of our boat across the labyrinthine shallows of Chatham Bar, as detailed in the following text, I have drawn our exact track on a 1977 aerial photograph of the area (see Appendix D). The differences between the hydrography as depicted in the photo and actual conditions during our sail two years earlier are minimal. The most significant difference is that the location identified on the photo

We sailed north for about a mile with no sign of a break in the combers. I then retraced my path to seek a break that perhaps I had missed on the first pass. Nothing. I sailed north again beyond the point where I had turned south the first time. Roy and I kept a close watch forward and aft to view the surf from every angle. Then we saw the break we were looking for. We had passed it by several hundred yards since it was not visible at a right angle to the beach. I sailed back to get a closer look. Where the break in the combers crossed the bar, I could see extremely shallow water. I was not sure we could get over that spot and was afraid of going hard aground in heavy, although not breaking, seas. As we loitered in the general area waiting for the fishing fleet to return, we continued to search for a better location to cross Chatham Bar. Then, at about 3:45 p.m., we saw the first fishing boat coming in. Hurray! We had our guides. We waited to see where that first boat would cross the bar.

The first boat bypassed the point I had identified as the best option and then turned into the surf several hundred yards south of us. The heavily loaded vessel progressed about halfway into the comber field and ran hard aground, seas breaking against her transom.

A second boat, not far behind the first, entered where I had intended to go. As it approached the shallow spot, it momentarily ran aground, and was immediately lifted over the bar by a surging sea into the deeper water beyond. Now convinced that was our best option, I headed into the cut, following in the wake of the second fishing boat.

---

where the second fishing boat ran aground for the second time appears to be less open for navigation in the photograph than it was two years earlier. Shifting sands appear to have further blocked that passage during the two-year interval.

A third boat had arrived on the scene and entered the surf at a third location running aground almost immediately.

The second boat had crossed the bar successfully but was aground a second time on an inner bar not visible from the open water.

Three fishing boats were aground on Chatham Bar as Roy and I committed to our entry. There was no turning back. Hard on the wind, breaking surf on either side, and propelled by the incoming ocean swells, we careened toward the shallow spot with frightening speed. The wind picked up sharply as we entered the "wind tunnel." I released the mainsheet allowing several feet to run out so the sail could spill the excess wind, enabling me to maintain control of the boat. The white noise of the wind and surf made voice communication impossible. Sliding down the back side of a surging sea into a trough, we slid across the shallow spot with a loud hiss as the keel scraped the sandy bottom. We were now inside the outer bar and outside the inner bar. Seas were breaking over the inner bar. We could not maintain our westerly heading without running aground on the inner bar. We had to turn either north or south. A right turn to the northwest took us in the general direction that we wanted to go, but navigable water dead-ended quickly onto dry beach. The low beach was hard to see from our dinghy-size boat over the breaking surf. Reversing direction, we beat to windward on a starboard tack against the southwesterly wind. Tacking to starboard (onto a port tack) to follow deep water, we searched for another break in the inner bar. Incoming combers were breaking on either side of us as we advanced along the relatively deep water channel between the two bars. As the breaking seas, coming in from the open ocean to our left, hit the deep water between the two bars, they relaxed into rolling swells until they broke again over the inner bar to our right.[3]

Continuing on a port tack, we headed directly into the path of the first boat that had dislodged itself from its first grounding and had run aground again on the inner edge of the outer bar just before breaking into the channel between the bars. That boat was to our left and only a few hundred feet ahead of us—almost directly in front of us. The boat's engine was at full power pushing it through the sand and inching the craft ever closer to freedom into the deep water channel between the bars. If it were to break loose as we passed under its bow, we would be history. But under we went within less than a boat's length from eternity.

Having passed that danger, we were presented with a dizzying array of alternately deep and shallow areas with no clear path to the deep, sheltering waters of Chatham Harbor and Pleasant Bay to the north. The channel westward was rapidly terminating. Some deeper water appeared to the north if we could only get beyond the inner bar that had risen to become a small island beach only about twenty yards to starboard. If we had to go aground, the closer we could get to the mainland beach the better. I slowly executed a hairpin turn to the right onto an easterly heading around the small island beach to our immediate right violently jibing the boat in the process. Again, deeper water appeared before us. The channel again seemed to end on a beach, but soon our changing perspective revealed a sharp turn in the channel to the north flanked on either side by dry sand to the right and impossible shallows to the left. Another desperate jibe flung us into that northbound leg. Dead ahead, at the end of the

---

[3]   The combers (breaking seas) through which we sailed do not appear in the Appendix D photo taken two years later under calmer conditions.

northbound leg of the channel, with Chatham Harbor only a few feet away on the other side, lay yet another shallow with less depth than the first one that we had encountered over the outer bar and upon which we had scraped our keel, but the deepest option available. I knew we could not get over this one. After all this effort, we were going to go hard aground within only a few feet of our goal. The wind, now about twenty-five to thirty knots, was behind us off the port quarter driving our boat headlong at that reef.

The lead keel hit the sand jolting us to a complete stop. The wind spun us around exposing the full area of sail to the direct blast of the wind. As we lay over on our side, water pouring into the cockpit, the boom dug into the sand preventing the sail from dumping its burden of air, a rising swell mercifully lifted the boat up and over the reef into the relatively calm, deep water of Chatham Harbor. Finally, at long last, we were across the bar in the safety of Chatham Harbor.

But the fun was not over. Heading north into a wide deep harbor, the press of sail threatened to capsize us with every gust. The free surface of water sloshing around in the cockpit did not help. We were so close to an anchorage that there was no point in reducing sail. Roy went forward to prepare the anchor. His weight on the bow, along with the force of wind on the sails, drove the bow down into the sea like a submarine headed for the deep. He jumped back, the bow popped up shedding water in every direction. The wind instantly caught the airborne water whipping it into a drenching spume that raked the deck and the two of us before vanishing over the whitecaps toward the beach. I turned the boat into the wind enough to allow Roy to prepare the anchor for deployment. Finding ourselves close to the base of Chatham light, we headed toward shore with the main and jib luffing violently but moving us forward. Easing the boat ever higher into the wind until she came to a stop, Roy dropped the anchor. I dropped the main, then the jib. In a moment of inattention, I let go of the main halyard after detaching it from the sail. The halyard blew out of reach streaming horizontally from the top of the mast. The boat was now stable at anchor, but the main halyard was flying from the masthead. We tried to reach it with an oar to no avail. The wind was unrelenting. We decided to leave the halyard as is and retrieve it the next day or whenever the wind calmed down enough to let the halyard drop to within reach. We secured the sails and gathered our things to go ashore. Everything was still perfectly dry inside the cabin although somewhat disheveled from being tossed about. We hauled the dinghy alongside. No water. The dinghy had somehow managed to stay dry throughout the fury of the day. Roy and I boarded the dinghy with one boat bag apiece and rowed ashore. After dragging the dinghy at least a hundred feet across the sand and securing it to a stable piece of driftwood well above the high tide line, we began the climb up the eighty-foot high sand bluff leading to a paved parking lot at the base of Chatham light. Hiking along the road into the town of Chatham for a mile or so, we came to the Cranberry Inn. There we found lodging, gin, good food, a hot shower, and soft beds. We had arrived in heaven. Thank you, God.

CHAPTER IV

RESCUE OFF RACE POINT

Following our wild ride across Chatham Bar to the base of the lighthouse high above on the sandy bluff, Roy and I, after hastily anchoring the boat, had left the halyard flying from the top of the mast in twenty-five-knot winds, unable to reach it to bring it down and secure it properly. Returning on the second day, we found the boat lying peacefully at anchor with the halyard swinging gently well within reach of human hands.

We had decided to leave on the outgoing tide hoping for the predicted SW breeze. The weather continued to grace us with gentle winds and bright sunshine. With boat bags in hand, we descended the steep bluff from Chatham Light to the beach. The dinghy, which we had dragged a considerable distance from the low tide mark to the driftwood to which we had tied it, was now only a few feet from the high water, an easy launch for the row out to the Bull's Eye.

Once out to the sailboat, we dipped our feet gingerly into the ocean to clear the soles of sand to keep the boat as clean as possible before climbing aboard. The first order of business was to grab and secure that halyard. Our fresh supply of clean clothes that we had laundered at a public Laundromat in Chatham were carefully stowed in the forward cuddy cabin along with a fresh supply of ice and sandwiches.

Most of the anchor line was pulled into the cockpit to shorten scope so that a minimum of line would have to be handled while getting under way. The main was raised taking care to keep the mainsheet from snagging any fittings and allowing the sail to fill prematurely driving the boat forward on the anchor. While I tended the mainsheet, Roy pulled more anchor line in to break the anchor free. He used the up and down motion of the boat in the waves to his advantage. When the boat went down, he pulled in the slack line and snubbed it on the cleat. When the boat went up, the strong force of the boat's buoyancy tugged the anchor upward out of its sandy burial. By repeating this process several times, the anchor was pulled free. I eased the boat forward being careful not to gain too much speed and bang the anchor against the hull. Roy sloshed the anchor up and down in the water until it was cleaned of sand and mud. He then brought the anchor, the three-foot length of chain, and the remainder of the anchor line onto the deck and into the cockpit, and we took off under full sail for the open sea. The short length of chain between the anchor and the anchor line protects the line from chafing on rocks, shells, and other bottom debris while anchored. The weight of the chain also keeps the pull on the anchor as horizontal as possible for anchoring efficiency. Too vertical a pull could prevent the anchor from grabbing the bottom while anchoring the boat and could pull the anchor free while anchored.

Crossing Chatham Bar was so easy at high tide; we barely noticed its existence. The offshore SW breeze left the sea as calm as if we were in Long Island Sound. With the breeze off our port quarter, we headed north for Provincetown. In fact, conditions were so perfect, we set the spinnaker which we carried for the rest of the afternoon and throughout the night.

Navigation was also easy along the east coast of the Cape. Lighthouses are spaced at about twelve-mile intervals permitting convenient triangulation to pinpoint our location as we proceeded along our route. We did get one surprise at about four o'clock in the morning. Race Point light suddenly went out. It just disappeared. We racked our brains to try and figure out what happened to that light. We finally concluded that a fog bank must have rolled in and obliterated the light. However, we were wrong. Had we looked more carefully at the chart, we would have seen that Race Point light is obscured from view for many miles due to the rising elevation of sand dunes along the outer Cape.

By dawn, fog had in fact settled in across the sea, so that we could not see much of anything. We doused the spinnaker and set the genoa to round Race Point on a progressively close reach into Provincetown. The wind was gentle, still from the southwest. Hours went by as we sailed on. By late morning the fog lifted, and we could see forever—forever in every direction—nothing but the empty horizon for 360 degrees. Where was the Cape? We had washed out to sea with the strong current ebbing out of Cape Cod Bay. We had no choice but to continue on until the tide changed and washed us back into the bay. I turned the boat onto the starboard tack, heading due south, to ensure that we would see land before passing so far north and west of Race Point that we miss it altogether.

By midafternoon, we sighted land, the current having changed a few hours earlier. The seas became sharper and higher but no more than three or four feet in height, indicating our entry into the rip off Race Point. About a mile offshore, we became aware of an odd activity in the water some distance ahead. Upon approaching this disturbance, we could see that it was a person in the water. I sailed gently up to the man sheltering him from the wave action with my lee side. Roy and I hauled him aboard along with his dive gear. The desperate fellow was scared to death. He had been diving from a small power boat and got swept out to sea in the strong rip current. When he came up, he was too far from his boat to signal for help and his tank was out of air. At least at this point he was washing back into the bay as were we. He pointed out his dive boat almost half a mile distant toward shore. As we sailed toward the boat we could see it circling, its panicked crew desperately looking for its lost diver. When the two men in the motorboat recognized their lost buddy in our boat, they made a beeline for us. I asked them to shut down so that I could make a landing on their boat. I approached upwind with my boom out to the side away from their boat. As we closed, the two boats began to move in unison on the waves. We used seat cushions as fenders between the two boats. With the boats tied together, the exhausted diver was transferred to the boat from whence he came, and three very relieved guys bonded with unbound exuberance. We quickly separated from the powerboat before any damage occurred in the seaway. As we sailed off we could hear thank-yous until out of earshot.

We reached Provincetown Harbor by early evening where we anchored close to the beach but at least a quarter mile from the town piers. A very long anchor rode was used to allow for a 9 to 11-foot rise and fall of tide in Provincetown Harbor. Lodging was readily found a short walk from the beach, and good restaurants were everywhere. Of course, the next day we climbed Pilgrim Monument and walked the many shops and artist's displays in town. At high noon, the town crier, dressed in period garb, walked from shop to shop poking his head into each store where he announced his presence with a large brass bell and, in a loud voice, proclaimed the latest news (or gossip) for one and all. Provincetown was a clean, quaint, and charming place.

CHAPTER V

A NIGHT IN PLYMOUTH JAIL

Roy and I shook hands as he prepared to depart. He wished me good luck, as I would venture on alone. His vacation time was over, and he had to return to work and his lead-engineer responsibilities at Pratt & Whitney, the jet engine maker in East Hartford, Connecticut. He left me his weather radio. As Roy walked away from the beach, I felt my heart race a little as I became acutely aware of being alone out there—really alone. I walked to the dinghy high and dry on the beach. Instead of walking to one side of the boat and grabbing the gunwale while Roy grabbed the other side, as we usually did, I walked to the bow and began to push alone. I really felt alone! The lightweight, hundred-pound dinghy seemed heavier than usual, but it began to slide across the sand and into the water. I threw in my boat bag and a bag of ice and shoved off. A short row brought me to the Bull's Eye, which seemed large and safe compared to the dinghy. Once aboard, I prepared to weigh anchor and set sail for Plymouth, some twenty-five miles distant across Cape Cod Bay.

All day I sailed on a close reach in bright sunshine and a warm, gentle breeze. I turned on Roy's weather radio and listened to a forecast of continued great weather. I began to feel less alone. In fact, I began to feel pretty damn good! I was king of the sea! I eased the mainsheet ever so gently until my weather helm disappeared but before any lee helm became evident. At that point I could leave the tiller long enough to get a sandwich out of the cooler and have lunch, minding the tiller every five minutes or so to keep on course. With a full belly and full sails, life was as good as it gets in a little boat in the middle of nowhere.

Based on my estimated progress, I would not make landfall until after dark, which was okay with me. As the sun set I could tell the night would be warm and friendly. I delayed until almost completely dark to turn on my running lights to conserve my six-volt battery. The heavy boat battery was strapped to the floor on the starboard side just inside the cuddy cabin adjacent to the center access door. With no engine, there was no way to charge the battery, so if the battery ran down, the light show was over. But the battery never did run down during the entire trip around Cape Cod. There was no boat traffic anywhere near me as I sailed into the sunset and into the night.

With the setting sun, I became progressively busier identifying shore navigation lights as they became visible. There had been a little crosscurrent both in and out of the bay during my crossing, which had almost no net effect on my track to Plymouth, so I was on course into the harbor. Depth perception at night is most deceptive. Navigation lights are white, red, or green. Red light has the longest wavelength and travels farthest through the atmosphere, which is why the setting sun looks red. Green has a shorter wavelength and is absorbed quickly by the atmosphere. The result is that green lights appear much farther away than they really are because they seem so dim compared to red lights that maintain their brightness for miles beyond their green counterparts. So a red and green pair of lights on either side of a channel entrance may seem totally disconnected from a distance, leading the sailor to believe that they are not the entrance markers when, in fact, they are. Knowing this little bit of trivia can really help sort things out at night.

As darkness set in, lights appeared everywhere. I needed to identify at least one of which I could be certain. The main harbor entrance was marked by a white light with a fifteen-mile range, which flashed three times every thirty seconds. I should be able to pick that one out among the maze of fixed and flashing lights visible from my position about four miles offshore. Shore lights having nothing to do with navigation, such as street lights, lights on buildings, and advertising signs contributed to the confusion. Nevertheless, I soon identified the triple white flasher and headed right for it. Plymouth's outer harbor is about a half mile wide and three miles long and is bound on either side by unlit banks of sand anywhere from awash to about a foot deep along its entire length. The sand rises above sea level much of that distance but cannot be seen in the blackness of the night. The far end of the outer harbor is marked by a flashing red light that gives out two flashes every five seconds. I already saw that. All I had to do, after I passed the white triple flasher on my starboard side, was to head directly for the double red flasher. This would be a no-brainer except for the fact that a strong ebbing current was drifting me from left to right. If I simply headed for the double red flasher, the current would wash me ashore onto the right bank long before I reached my target. Adding to the challenge was a westerly breeze coming from exactly where I wanted to go. Since sailboats don't go directly into the wind, I would have to tack back and forth at a forty-five-degree angle to the wind to make progress upwind. But how far left and right could I go without going aground as I tacked upwind? In order to determine that limit, I had to study the chart. Still in open water, I abandoned the tiller, grabbed a flashlight, and let the boat go wherever it wanted. While the boat sailed itself, I used a protractor, made for airplane course plotting, to establish a course line of 263 degrees from the triple white flasher to the target double red flasher. I could not sail to the right of that line due to the close proximity of the sand banks, but I had at least a quarter of a mile leeway of safe deep water to the left of that line for the entire three-mile stretch to the double red flasher. I determined that if I sailed on a starboard tack to the left of and away from my course line, my bearing to the red flasher would steadily increase from 263 at my course line to 268 degrees at the quarter mile limit, a total of +5 degrees. At that point I would come about onto a port tack and return to my 263 degree course line. This process would repeat until I reached the double red flasher. Since each tack would bring me closer to the red flasher, my bearing to it at the quarter-mile limit would be one or two degrees greater than the previous tack until, at very close range, the red flasher would appear on a bearing of 263+15 degrees or 278 degrees. In order to stay within my safety band of deep water, I would have to use my "hockey puck" hand bearing compass to track my position relative to my target red flasher as I sailed. With a self-tacking jib, all I had to do was steer the boat and mind my bearing with the hockey puck held up to my eye as I sailed along. Whew! That seemed awfully complicated just to sail into a wide open harbor. But at night, with a strong cross current and a headwind, I would be lucky to make it at all without running aground. I had to pay attention and make no serious mistakes. Fortunately, I was too busy to think much about that. The pressure of that challenging nighttime entry into Plymouth Harbor kept me on edge, focused, and alert. A GPS would have made this so simple, but alas, such navigational wonders did not exist in the early 1970s, so I soldiered on with my basic instruments.

The first mile into the harbor was the easiest. As I passed the white triple flasher to my right, three green lighted buoys to my left guided me into the harbor. Then nothing but blackness spread before me for the next two miles except for my target double red flasher at the far end. I could feel the effect of the cross current on my track. A long tack to the left was necessary to reach my five-degree limit in that direction because the current was pushing me to the right. When I tacked back to the right onto the port tack (wind from the left side), I reached my 263 degree course line alarmingly fast. I had to keep my hockey puck compass up to my eye almost constantly to control my position in the channel. As I got closer to my goal, I increased my allowance on each starboard tack from +5 degrees to +7, then +10, and finally to +15 degrees. At that point I was almost on top of the double red flasher, and I had not run aground. I felt safe at last, at least for the moment.

Having reached the double red flashing light, I began to circle around to study my chart for the next leg into the inner harbor. The wind was light enough to allow me to let the boat jibe or tack as I circled without serious disturbance. Although the channel into the inner harbor was quite narrow, it was well marked and would be easy to follow. Best of all, I would no longer have to tack. All I had to do was set out in the right direction to get started. Getting started in the right direction was particularly important since the channel markers were all unlit requiring the use of a beam light to pick up their reflecting tapes. My launching point would be, of course, the double red flasher. When I looked up to reorient myself with the red flashing light, it was gone! Gone! That was not possible! How could it be gone?! All of a sudden, I felt totally disoriented in the suffocating darkness expecting at any moment to be washed aground by the swift current. Then I saw a white light flashing. What the hell was that? It was not on the chart. I looked back down at the chart to see if I had missed a major light. At that moment the boat lurched as the boom swung around in a sharp jibe snapping the sheet tight at the end of its travel, this in response to my circling down wind. I heard my flashlight roll off the seat onto the cockpit floor. I dove after it fumbling in the dark. Precious seconds lost while I groped the floor chasing after the lost light. Frustration built as I tried to maintain position near the lights hoping to somehow not run aground. Recovering the flashlight, I found nothing on the chart about a white flashing light near the red one. Looking up again, there was the red flasher as if nothing had happened. This was crazy. Was I so fatigued that I was hallucinating? Noticing that I had drifted away from the light, I turned my attention back to my boat to sail it closer to the light. This maneuver placed my back to the light. When I again looked toward the light, all I saw was the white flasher. Were there two lights, one obscured by the other? Was this a red sector light? My chart said no. Besides, a red sector light would make no sense here. Now I was getting panicky. This whole situation made no sense to me at all. The light was red again. Jesus, help me!

I circled aimlessly in the vicinity of the lights trying to get myself together. As I did so I noticed the light color changing as I circled around and around and sailed back and forth. Contributing to my inability to figure this puzzle out was the fact that the red and white lights appeared to be separated by some distance from each other. This, as it turned out, was just an illusion caused by my motion through the water in total darkness coupled with the five-second dark interval between flashes. With no other land based visual references close to the lights, the red and the white never seemed to be in the same place twice. Eventually, I tumbled to the possibility that the two lights may in fact be on the same structure and that their apparent separation was an illusion caused by the boat's motion. Then it hit me—of course! A panel must be broken or missing in the lamp. The lamp must be a white light surrounded by red-colored glass panels. I suddenly felt so stupid! But at least I understood that the red and white flashing lights were one and the same. I set my course from the red/white flasher to the inner harbor channel entrance and immediately picked up the first buoy reflector in my beam light. From there I hopped from buoy to buoy for about two miles until the channel ended at the famous Plymouth Rock. There, in the quiet little enclave, I anchored and dropped my sail. Another leg successfully, albeit painfully, completed.

Gathering my things that I would need ashore—my boat bag—I loaded them into my loyal little dinghy that had so obediently followed me throughout my dizzy, tail-chasing entry into this place. I rowed ashore and tied the dinghy to the nearest solid object. I have no recollection whatever of exactly what it was

I tied up to, but the dinghy was still there the next day. I began to walk. Finding myself on a street in the town of Plymouth, I became acutely aware of my surroundings. The short dinghy ride had transcended me from a vast watery desert, unsheltered from the earlier sun and wind, and later, the seemingly impenetrable darkness, the smell of salt air, the endless, grueling motion of my small boat, the incessant white noise of the sea, and the unceasing demand to sail the boat and to navigate while remaining alert at all times to some level of ever present danger ready to blind side the unsuspecting lone sailor without warning; to another world with tall, leafy trees that rose silently on either side of the street and stirred with the soft flutter of summer leaves. The captivating smell of dense foliage and flowers, the solid feel of the ground under my feet all felt so safe and reassuring. Occasional street lights broke the darkness. The streets were deserted with attractive homes and sleeping shops visible through the shadows on either side. I could walk freely in any direction without worrying about jibing the boom or tacking upwind. Life was suddenly so wonderfully simple and relaxing! The contrast between the active, demanding ocean and the tranquil, secure landscape enthralled me to distraction. I was still dressed for offshore sailing in my long cotton pants, bright yellow foul weather jacket, and white safety harness with its five-foot tether dangling in a swaying loop from the harness, and the boat bag getting heavier by the minute. My watch showed 1:00 a.m. I thought I might lie down right there on the grass and go to sleep for the night. No one would notice.

A pair of headlights broke my reverie from a distance around a bend in the road, the first car I had seen since coming ashore. I stood and watched as they approached. Characteristic running lights on the roof identified the vehicle as a patrol car. I knew it would not pass me by. The cruiser stopped next to me. The window came down, and I heard from the shadowy figure within, "Can I help you?"

"I just sailed over from Provincetown in a sixteen-foot boat, and I'm looking for a place to stay."

"Get in and we'll look together."

Sitting in the soft seat of the police car felt so good; I thought I might go to sleep before we covered half a mile. I began relating the events of my odyssey around the Cape. My driver was fascinated by all he heard and began firing questions one after another until we reached the police station. Several of the inns we passed were, of course, closed. The officer, now a true buddy, invited me into the station and offered me a seat and newspaper to read. Seeing me nodding off and dropping the paper, he ventured, "Would you like to try one of my special accommodations?"

"I thought you would never ask," I replied.

We both laughed as I stood up and walked heavily over to one of two spotlessly clean cells where he had already unlocked and opened the door. I lay down on the clean Naugahyde cot in the middle of the cell. A clean white porcelain sink occupied one corner, a commode another. Lying on my back, looking up at the ceiling, the oppressive weight of my foul weather jacket, harness and tether aggravated me, but I was too tired to do anything about them. I heard the door clink shut and fell asleep under the bright lights in the cell.

Clink, clank! I opened my eyes with a start, saw bars all about me, and struggled to a sitting position trying to remember how and why I got imprisoned there. Sunlight filled the room. A uniformed man stood in the open cell door laughing at my obvious distress and saying something about eight o'clock. As it all came back to me, my face flushed with embarrassment to the officer's further amusement.

After a cup of coffee and some conversation about my plans for the day, the officer, still on duty, directed me to a breakfast shop nearby. After dropping my foul weather jacket and harness in the dinghy, I found the eatery and restoked the furnace of life. Sailing across Cape Cod Bay, through the Cape Cod Canal, and up a narrow estuary to Onset, Massachusetts was the next order of business. Returning to my boat, I began to study my charts and Eldridge to time my entry into the swift, swirling currents of the canal.

CHAPTER VI

ENCOUNTERS IN THE CAPE COD CANAL

Sailing through the Cape Cod Canal without an engine is strictly prohibited by law (and adult common sense). However, that was not about to deter me from completing my planned circumnavigation of the Cape. All I wanted to do was to ensure that my entry into the canal was with both the wind and the current. I would not leave Plymouth until those two planets aligned.

The wind was blowing moderately from the northeast. The sun was shining in a mostly cloudless sky. Roy's weather radio was predicting stormy weather a few days out with the NE wind continuing and slowly increasing as the storm approached. The current in the canal, according to Eldridge, would turn to the west about 12:30 p.m. in my favor. The planets were aligned, and I would be late if I left immediately, but not too late. I still had some ice in the cooler, an apple, water, and a Coke and part of an old ham and cheese sandwich—not ideal, but good enough.

Weighing anchor and setting sail single-handedly is always a challenge, even under the best of conditions. Except for somewhat tight quarters in the protected inlet where I was anchored, I had the best of conditions. Cleaning the anchor off after pulling it off the bottom, while the boat drifts and the sails begin to catch air, is the trickiest part of the job; but all went well, and I was off. After about a mile of short tacks along the narrow channel, I was able to sail freely out of the harbor and into Cape Cod Bay. With a strong ten-to-fifteen-knot breeze on my port beam and a fair current, the little Bull's Eye charged toward the canal at about five knots. Close to four hours after leaving Plymouth, I entered the eastern end of the 7.5-mile land cut. The time was 2:00 p.m., approximately an hour and a half into my five-hour tidal current window.

The canal snakes through the state of Massachusetts severing it from the Cape Cod peninsular and connecting Cape Cod Bay at the eastern end to Buzzards Bay to the west in a long, lazy, S-shaped curve. That geography eventually became operative, as I sailed farther into the canal, by increasingly sheltering me from the breeze that drove me forward. Although the current would continue to move me forward, without the wind I would have no maneuverability in the canal to keep my boat out of harm's way.

For the moment I scudded along unimpeded. The shore was lined for miles with people fishing or just walking. Many waved as I went by. Seeing a small sailboat in the canal was most certainly a rare sight. I kept as close to the shore as I dared to avoid being surprised by a large ship going up the center, but there was none. A few small power boats passed in either direction. Some people called out to me from the shore, but I could not hear much of what they said. I returned waves and shouts of greeting. Scenic overlooks, for unseen automobile traffic adjacent to the canal, poked out from the tree-lined banks here and there. This was really fun!

My boat twisted back and forth as I sailed through large whirlpools in the swirling five-to-six-knot current. Those whirlpools were not like the deep-centered whirlpools that go down a bathtub drain. Instead, they were defined by deep, circular tucks around their peripheries that could suck a swimmer down and under the surface. The whirlpools were anywhere from four to twenty feet in diameter. I could see the large flat rocks that lined the cut to form the canal in the clear deep water below the boat. A zing of tightness gripped my stomach as I realized the futility of trying to engage any of those smooth rocks with my anchor to prevent drifting into the center of the canal should I lose the wind. The possibility of being dragged into the path or wake of a large passing ship with no way to stop induced the pang of fear, along with the realization that I was beyond the point of no return in the swift current. But the sun was warm and bright, and the breeze strong and steady—not to worry!

My attention was soon diverted by the appearance of a large white vessel rounding a bend behind me in the canal. A second look revealed the unmistakable red, white, and blue stripes of a coast guard vessel. As it passed, I continued to wave to the crowds on the shore with my back to the boat. The CG skipper passed me by, stopped, and began to reverse. This was not good. The CG boat was a large cutter; I estimated to be a good eighty feet in length. I reasoned that if I stayed very close to the banks of the canal, he would not dare venture close enough to inspect me and risk running his deep-draft cutter onto a rock. I kept my back to him so that he could not signal me visually to sail over to him for an inspection to verify that I had the required engine. I prayed that he would not call me over with an electric-powered hailer. A five- or six-minute eternity went by with the CG cutter not moving relative to me. Glancing over my shoulder, I was stunned to see a man on the deck staring at me through large binoculars! I again turned my back to him and continued to wave at the people. I had to diffuse the situation somehow. I could not risk an inspection, but how could I get him to go? I knew that he could see every detail on my boat along with the dinghy that I was towing, my offshore sailing gear, my binoculars and hockey puck, life vest and harness, everything but my charts that were hidden in the cockpit. So I raised one of them as if to study it so that he could see that as well. I wanted to create the impression that I was so well equipped that I had to know what I was doing and would certainly have an inboard engine in my sturdy little boat. The suspense was killing me. I finally turned to face him directly, gave him a big wave too and a broad smile. He put his binoculars down, returned the big wave, and hustled back into his wheelhouse. The cutter bolted forward and disappeared. That was close!

I passed under the beautiful Sagamore Bridge, one of the two automobile traffic suspension bridges linking the mainland to the Cape. The roadway passed 135 feet overhead, the support structure towering another one hundred feet, or so, above that— truly an impressive sight from below!

About halfway through the land cut portion of the canal—the additional portion being a defined channel extending for several miles into Buzzards Bay and marked by large buoys, which is legally part of the canal—I began noticing a reduction in wind speed but nothing to be concerned about. The shore had become mostly deserted, the crowds of friendly people nowhere to be seen. I passed under the Bourne Bridge, the second of the two roadways onto the Cape and identical to the first. Then I came upon the railroad bridge, the lone rail link to the Cape about a mile beyond the Bourne Bridge and could see that it was in the raised position. That was fortunate since in the lowered position there is only a seven-foot clearance under it—not quite enough to clear my twenty-two-foot mast. And with a five-to six-knot current sweeping me inexorably toward the bridge, there would be no escaping being swept into it. This is another reason not to traverse the canal without an engine—the inability to anchor and the fact that it is against the law in the first place, being the first two.

Beyond the railroad bridge, the canal begins to open up into Buzzards Bay. As I left the land cut portion of the canal behind and entered the marked channel, the wind had all but vanished. At that point, I was mostly drifting out into the bay and centered in the five-hundred-foot wide channel. At last I could begin to relax as the waterway widened into the bay. Unwittingly allowing myself to drift into the center of the channel was another mistake for which I nearly paid dearly. I noticed a high-powered motor craft with a black hull approaching from the open bay as if to enter the canal in the opposite direction against the current. This boat was going to pass me fairly closely. No, it was heading for me and slowing down. As it approached, I could see, in large, white, block letters on the side of the hull, "ARMY CORPS OF ENGINEERS." I was about to be inspected, after all, by the supervising authority for the canal.

As the patrol boat neared, a man stepped out of the wheelhouse and, looking down at me, yelled, "You better get out of the canal!" adding, "Look behind you!" I spun around to see a huge tanker emerging from the land cut into the channel and bearing down on us with a bone in its teeth! I looked back at him in obvious shock. He growled, "Start your engine and move out of the canal!" Then he stood there staring down at me waiting for me to comply. Still unable to admit my scofflaw status and foolishly choosing gamesmanship and vanity over safety, I reached down under my seat on the port side with my left hand, and as I whipped my tiller over to port with my right hand to nudge the boat into a right turn toward the edge of the channel, I began to rattle my anchor chain against the inside of the Bull's Eye's hull with my left hand to simulate the sound of an engine. That's all he had to hear. With the tanker bearing down on us, he had no inclination to hang around any longer. He turned his back and bolted into his wheelhouse, gunned his engine, and disappeared back into the bay leaving me wallowing in his hilly wake, my sails slatting back and forth uselessly. For the briefest of moments I felt so slick! I had evaded another authority. He was out of my way…but not the tanker. Had I surrendered my life for my pride? What a fool was I!

With every glance over my shoulder, the tanker loomed closer and larger and seemed to be coming at me faster and faster. I could have climbed into my dinghy and towed the Bull's Eye out of harm's way, but there was no time. I grabbed one of my oars from the dinghy and paddled for my life toward the edge of the channel. I could hear the leviathan parting the sea to get at me. I paddled. The ship seemed so wide! I paddled. I was clear! The ship blocked the sun as her bow slid past like a freight train. Although the underbodies of large ships are designed to minimize the size of their bow waves and stern wakes as they move through the water, the surface around them is, nevertheless, severely traumatized. At one end of the ship, a huge volume of water equal to the ship's total displacement is parted and pushed aside only to be cataclysmically rejoined at the other end where the wake is further roiled by huge propellers releasing thousands of horsepower into the sea in a corkscrew pattern to drive the ship forward. I could feel the bow wave pushing me away as the ship passed a mere seventy-five to one hundred feet distant. I could see every detail of the giant steel plates as they passed by—weld seams with rust bleeding out onto the faded black paint, rivet heads that I could have used as anchors, heavy skid marks from contact with piers, and black rubber fenders (truck tires). The deck was so high that I could see none of the superstructure. As the ship passed, I drifted closer to her stern, her wake beginning to suck me in. Again, I paddled. I felt my little boat swing around the stern of the ship as it sped forward, clearing me by little more than fifty feet. I could feel the rhythmic thudding of her single screw sending hydraulic pressure pulses upward into my hull. The sea churned all about me with surprisingly little effect on my boat. From my vantage well into, but not centered in, the ship's wake, I watched the tanker and me part company as rapidly as we had met.

A slight breeze had come up. I set my sails to meet it and headed out of the channel for the mile-and-a-half-long waterway into Onset, the entry to which was almost on top of my current position. While heading for the first beacon, I began to think about the day's events. This had not been a stellar day. I don't think I ever had a day strewn with more mistakes of seamanship and bad judgments in all my years of sailing. God had been more than kind to me for allowing me to survive it all unscathed. If anything can be learned from my experiences in the Cape Cod Canal, it is this:

1. Don't ever enter the Cape Cod Canal, or similar waterway, under sail alone without some kind of an engine.
2. Obey the laws. Your life may depend on it.
3. Always look around you, 360 degrees, to know what may be coming at you.
4. Be especially alert in shipping lanes.

There may be more, but that will do for starters.

The waterway to Onset is as narrow as a lane between docks in a typical marina. Traffic moved in both directions. Of course, I had the only boat under sail. That annoyed a few boaters, but fascinated most, my dinghy, charts and other offshore gear bearing witness to a long open-water passage.

The narrow channel opened up into a small anchorage in the town of Onset. I located one of several open mooring buoys and made an easy landing. The best indication that an empty mooring is available is that no dinghy is tied up to it. Most people do not tow the dinghy when they go out for a sail. They leave the dinghy tied up to the mooring. I picked up the mooring pennant and secured it to my bow cleat, dropped the main, and looked around. What a pretty little town! Continuing to secure the boat, I prepared to leave in my dinghy for the short row ashore. Once on the short, steep beach, I tied the dinghy to a tree and walked up the embankment to the sidewalk.

As usual, having no idea where to go, I began to walk toward the most bustling area of commercial activity looking around for a place to stay. And again, as usual, I soon found such a place. A particularly clean and well-kept inn took my notice, and through the front door I went. Nobody was around, but I could hear construction noises on the second floor. Up I went in pursuit of the source of that industrious sound. Upon entering a room, a young couple, surprised by my sudden appearance, turned toward me and stopped working. The lady broke the silence. "Hello! We are not open yet, but we will be in a few days."

"I am traveling in a small sailboat, and am looking for a place to stay. Your inn is beautiful. I would be honored to be your first guest. I do not need any special services or food, just a place to put my sleeping bag and access to a shower. The construction activity and dust will not bother me at all, and I will be happy to pay the price of a room."

The man and his wife, covered with sanding dust from head to toe, looked at each other through dust-covered eyelashes, then back at me. Again the woman spoke. "I can give you a room on the first floor if you don't mind the dust and noise. We will have to keep working to open on time."

"Thank you, this is exciting!" I countered, my boyish enthusiasm spilling over. With that she showed me to my room, lovingly decorated with a beautiful antique bed and furnishings. She gave me a set of towels, directed me to the bath, and returned to her work. I was given no key, having been informed that none was required. Taking all of two minutes to settle in, I went back out onto the street and looked up the harbor master to pay for my mooring, three dollars for the night.

I never did eat that old ham and cheese sandwich. So after having only the apple and Coke all day, I was ready—more than ready—for some real food, which I found but a short distance from where I stood thinking about it.

In the morning, the lady of the house invited me to join her and her husband in her kitchen for coffee and pastry—a wonderful start to what was to become a memorable day, and night, to say the least. Upon hearing my short synopsis, in a few thousand well-chosen words, of adventure on the high seas, she insisted on supplying me with more breakfast—ham and eggs—and a sandwich, pear, and pastry to sustain me during the long trek to Harwich Port, Massachusetts.

CHAPTER VII

CAUGHT IN A FISH TRAP

The stormy weather that I had been watching for a couple of days was due in by nightfall. The predictions were for Small Craft Warnings and high winds with little, if any, rain. That was not a particular concern for me because I would be ending my trip in familiar waters that I had plied since childhood, and I had sailed my boat in such conditions many times before, including shrieking, forty-five-knot winds in Fishers Island Sound near Noank, Connecticut. I was more concerned with threading my way through the shallow, reef-littered coastal waters of Nantucket Sound at night where few lighted buoys existed to guide me. Shore-based beacons were plentiful and would serve me well for triangulating my positions, but floating lights, in addition to the fixed, land-based lights, would have enabled me to more accurately pinpoint my exact locations as I sailed.

A gentle breeze out of the—everywhere—eased me along the channel from Onset back into Buzzards Bay. The surrounding trees and man-made structures swirled air at me from every conceivable direction causing my boom to jibe from side to side or the sail to luff without notice. The average direction seemed to be mostly from the northeast as predicted. There was little current in the channel to bother me, and the early morning boat traffic was light.

The sun was bright, the air warm, the day gorgeous! Veering off to starboard into the bay, the little Bull's Eye leaned and strained under the press of sail pulling me ever faster into open water. A quartering wind and following sea, along with a fair current, whisked me on my way toward the Cape mainland town of Woods Hole about fifteen nautical miles distant and halfway down Buzzards Bay. My little dinghy, like a puppy bouncing with energy it doesn't know what to do with, kept charging at my stern as if to take a nip out of it. So I let out its leash to give it more playroom. This made it very happy. The happy sailor, with his happy dinghy in tow, yelled with delight at no one in particular. Then came a verse or two from the movie, *Twenty Thousand Leagues Under the Sea*: "Got a whale of a tale to tell you lads, a whale of a tale or two, 'bout the girls I've loved with the moon above, a whale of a tale and it's all true, I swear by my tattoo." Life was good! No spray was coming aboard to dampen the party, even in the three-to-four-foot seas. Going to windward or on a close reach would have been an entirely different matter.

I could plainly see from a private consultation with my trusty Eldridge that the current past Woods Hole would turn against me before I got there. The restricted Woods Hole Passage, pressed between the port of Woods Hole on the northern side of the passage, and the north end of the Elizabeth Island chain that separates Buzzards Bay from Vineyard Sound to the south of the passage, accelerates the tidal current to speeds exceeding five knots.

Navigation was easy on that bright, sunny, clear day allowing me to find the buoy marking the entrance to Woods Hole Passage without the use of my binoculars. The seas quieted down as I entered Woods Hole Passage, but the current increased against me. The wind held steady at about twelve to fifteen knots. I pulled the dinghy in closer to avoid the risk of clipping a channel marker buoy should we pass that close to one. On either side of the passage, Mother Nature had deposited one of her many rock collections for all to plainly see and admire. Keeping my boat strategically positioned in the passage channel so that if I lost wind, I would not wash into or over any of dear Mother's cherished collectibles and—God forbid—scratch one of them as I destroyed my boat, was a Level 1 priority.

Well into the passage channel, my progress slowed and slowed. I watched the channel markers come to an almost complete stop, relative to my boat, as the water raced past my hull. Is this how I was going to spend the day, waiting for the current to slacken, so that I could pass into Vineyard Sound and on into Nantucket Sound? Each time the wind slowed ever so slightly, my progress would stop. Several times the current overpowered the wind forcing me to lose ground, which I then made up in the gusts. One huge buoy, weighing several tons and only a few yards away to starboard, swayed back and forth menacingly, as it lay almost completely horizontal in the raging current. By making careful adjustments to my sails and adjusting the dinghy so that it was riding down my wake wave to minimize its drag, I inched forward through the pinch point of the passage into the Vineyard Sound end of the waterway. Several hours had been consumed fighting the current in Woods Hole Passage. The midafternoon sun was hot, and the wind began to die. Many more miles lay ahead before this day could end. For several more hours I sailed against a two-to three-knot current in the transition region between Vineyard and Nantucket Sounds. Gradually, both the wind and the current dropped off to almost nothing. The time was about 5:00 p.m. I was tired and hungry.

A ferry boat coming into Woods Hole passed by only a few hundred yards away. I watched her wake approach my low rail and remember thinking, "That wake will come aboard if I don't do something." I continued to stare at it like a deer in headlights. And guess what – it marched right aboard giving me a good soaking and getting everything wet. What an ass! Well, that shook me out of my reverie. But when I tried to move to clean up the mess, I barely had enough energy to drag myself off the seat. I became dizzy, then nauseous when I did start to move. Momentarily panicked by my unexpected helplessness and sudden, intense awareness of how alone I was out there, I feared for my life. At the same time, I realized that the heat of the day had sapped all the energy out of me to a dangerous level. I was salt deficient—a problem that could have been easily solved with a few small sips of seawater, two or three gallons of which were sloshing about me in the cockpit. I was also dehydrated from not drinking enough fluids. I was in trouble. I crawled across the cool, wet cockpit floor, which felt so refreshing, to the open door of the cuddy cabin and drank some of the ice water in the bottom of the cooler, then a V-8 and a Coke and quickly began to feel much better. I devoured the wonderful care package, wrapper and all—just kidding—so generously provided by my hostess in Onset. With renewed strength and energy, I dried the cockpit and began to plot my way across Nantucket Sound toward Harwich Port, my physical and psychological trauma of mere minutes ago now ancient history.

The sun was getting lower in the sky; 7:00 p.m. had come and gone. Precious little daylight remained. I had to get as far as I could with the remaining daylight and position myself safely for the dark excursion along the reef-laden waters of Nantucket Sound. The wind had turned to the northwest over my port quarter and was quickly picking up speed. Thickening clouds had gathered in the sky. The night was going to be dark, very dark. The moon and Milky Way would not be visible to cast helpful light. In anticipation of increasing wind and seas, I let the dinghy out to the full extent of its forty-foot painter.

In the fading daylight the seas had already built to about four feet, driven by wind that had picked up to a good twelve knots. The following seas would sneak up under the stern of the dinghy lifting it high into the air. The dinghy would then cascade down the waves like an errant surfboard passing the Bull's Eye until yanked to a halt at the end of its tether. Unfortunately, the larger the seas got, the farther they would surf the dinghy past the larger boat. Sometimes the dinghy would snap its tether tight from abeam causing a sharp tug at right angles to the dinghy's centerline. With the painter attached to the dinghy at the top of the stem (deck level), the sideways tug had a tendency to roll the boat over on its side. I had never seen the dinghy pulled completely over, but this tendency concerned me as the seas were steepening and breaking into whitecaps.

With darkness creeping over the sea, I lost more and more visual detail. Soon, all I could see around the boat were the foaming tops of the waves as the curling action energized the phosphorescence of living organisms in the water causing the breaking crests to literally glow in the dark. I could no longer see the dinghy. I had laid out my navigation tools and charts so that I could find everything in the dark. The red and green navigation lights on either side of the cuddy cabin revealed only the lower portion of the shrouds and a small patch of green deck and teak toe rail in their soft glow. I could also see occasional drops of spray whipping across the deck past the red running light on the high, port side, and the gurgling sea sliding past the green light, low and close to the water due to the boat's heel, on the starboard side. The glow of the white stern light on the first few feet of the dinghy painter revealed the general direction of that little boat at all times. The quartering seas and wind kept the dinghy off to starboard for the most part. The Bull's Eye's wake was aglow all around me with blue phosphorescence in bright little whirlpools and other patches of energized water. The sails were barely visible, but eventually, the blackness swallowed them whole. The white numbers on the floating compass card in the center of the boat were clearly visible with a pink glow under the red light of the compass dome as was the fixed lubber line (vertical pin) indicating the boats heading. The illuminated compass card seemed to be suspended in midair surrounded by nothing but darkness. Beyond and around the boat itself, the sea and sky became a uniform black void with no horizon and few stars to be seen. With so much darkness and no stable references, other than the compass card and the distant shore lights, I struggled to maintain a sense of horizontal. Only the stable, gimbaled compass card kept me mentally on plane while the boat surged up and down in the building seaway, unless I looked over at the distant shore lights, which provided instant reorientation. Vertigo was a clear and present danger, especially while looking down at my charts.

Knowing my position at all times among those reefs was absolutely essential—more important, in fact, than making progress. So I was determined not to move forward unless I knew exactly where I was going to be moving forward from. But then how does one not move under sail? Elementary, my dear Watson; one heaves to. Heaving to usually, but not always, is accomplished by back-winding the jib and adjusting the main to drive against the back-winded jib, such that, the boat sits in the water at about a forty-five-degree angle to the wind. When properly set, the mainsail will be luffing. Pulling in the main will move the boat forward; letting it out will allow the back-winded jib to drive the boat slowly aft and off the wind. The tiller is allowed to swing free or is tied off center to turn the boat into the wind. Every boat is somewhat different, so this technique must be experimented with and practiced in controlled conditions before it can be reliably applied in a situation like this. In the dark and in a rough sea, determining if the boat is moving forward or backward is not easy. Only the body language of the boat will confirm if it is stable in a heaved-to state. A slight scalloping action may occur, as the boat falls off, then turns into the wind, stalls and falls off again. Some drifting through the water will result, and any existing tidal current will also sweep the boat along with it, so one must remain vigilant to some movement over the ground (sea floor) while heaved to.

Heaving to for the first time that night set the boat up to take spray over the cockpit. Fortunately, most of the water passed overhead and into the sea on the other side. I was able to work on my knees in the cockpit using the port (windward) seat as a table for my chart while somewhat sheltered from the weather by the Bull's Eye's hull as she heeled slightly to leeward. The chart was encased in a large clear vinyl envelope to protect it from the water and to give it enough heft to stay aboard. Light was provided by a flashlight containing a bulb that I had painted with red nail polish to emit the requisite night vision-saving red-colored light.

Using my hockey puck hand bearing compass, I took my first reading of a shore-based beacon that I could also identify on my chart. I then slid the chart part way out of its protective enclosure and drew a pencil line from the subject beacon in the direction indicated by my reading. I repeated this process with a different beacon. Where the two pencil lines crossed was my position. Once again, I repeated the process using a third beacon. The third line did not pass through the point where the first two lines intersected. Instead, the third line missed that point by about a half inch (equivalent to a half mile on the ocean). That result was not acceptable since it indicated an error of up to a half mile. I had to start again using the same three beacons. Holding the hand bearing compass steady while I took my readings was difficult in the heaving boat and was the main source of inaccuracy. After a few iterations, I reduced the size of the triangle formed by the three intersecting lines. Finally, with some semblance of confidence in my readings, I was ready to resume sailing. But how far could I go before having to stop and navigate again? Based on the proximity of the surrounding reefs, I estimated that I could travel about a mile safely before having to stop and navigate. At an estimated boat speed of four to five knots, I would cover one mile in about twelve to fifteen minutes. Having just spent twenty-five minutes heaved to and navigating to determine my position, I could only sail for about fifteen minutes, at most, before having to stop and navigate again to confirm my new position. Hopefully, my navigation sessions would become more efficient, so that I could reduce each one to fifteen or twenty minutes in duration. In short, the best I could expect was to sail for fifteen and navigate for fifteen. Not ideal, but safety demanded the discipline of such a schedule and routine.

As an interesting side note, my hockey puck hand bearing compass was illuminated for night use by a light-emitting tritium gas capsule, which was most effective. Likewise, my self-winding Bulova wristwatch was illuminated by a radium dial that had bits of radium on the numbers and hands to reveal the time. The illumination lasted all night. Today, both tritium and radium, being mildly radioactive, are banned from such uses.

During my second navigating session, I determined that I had traveled slightly farther than I had anticipated. Remembering the time of changing tidal current in the sound, I realized that a gentle current was carrying me in the desired direction of travel—a welcome break. Once again I sailed on.

Bump! What was that? I wheeled around toward the direction of the hit just in time to see my white dinghy retreating like the head of a great white shark from the transom that it had just hit, evidence that the seas were continuing to build and the wind increasing. The surfing dinghy was becoming more unruly, yanking at its leash with disturbing violence. But none of that could I see unless a sea fired the little boat directly at me bringing it to within range of the glow of my stern light or, as in this case, actually hitting the Bull's Eye from behind. More direct hits were to come, none of which I could prevent, and all of which startled me.

Having successfully passed the rocky Succonnessett and Wreck Shoals to port and the equally treacherous Horseshoe Shoal to starboard, I breathed a little easier as their one-to-ten-foot shallows fell away safely astern. Nantucket Sound was opening up, to my joyful relief, with wider, deeper water. My joy and relief were short-lived!

A powerful tug from astern sent me sprawling onto the cockpit floor. The boat came to an abrupt halt as if run aground. I could not have run aground in sixty-foot deep water! Gathering myself up, I made my way back to the aft deck. There, I could see the dinghy painter pulled as tight as an anchor line in a good blow. In fact, that is exactly what I had, an anchor—a sea anchor! The dinghy had swamped in the large seas and was holding the Bull's Eye fast as if it had hooked a lobster pot buoy. I let out the main and jib sheets to dump air from the sails and then turned the boat into the wind as far as she would go with the dinghy pulling at her stern. With the swamped dinghy holding the stern into the wind, the partially filled, luffing sails continued to pull the boat slowly forward on what amounted to a broad, almost beam, reach. I returned aft, grabbed the dinghy painter, and began to pull. Slowly, hand-over-hand, I managed to pull the dinghy to within view. I was shocked to see her wallowing below the surface like a great fish on the end of a line. At least her floatation kept her at or near the surface. But now what? I could not hold onto the line forever. So lying on my stomach with my thighs hooked over the short aft deck into the cockpit to ensure that I stayed aboard, I tried to pull the nose of the dinghy up and out of the water where I could grab it with both hands. I found that, with great effort, I could roll the dinghy over into an upright position and lift the bow, which allowed much of the water to slosh out as the Bull's Eye surged forward feeling the reduced drag. By pulling the bow of the dinghy high into the air, I was able to empty almost two-thirds of the water out of it. I then let the dinghy gradually out to the full extent of its painter and returned to sailing the boat. Even with the dinghy still almost half full of water, the Bull's Eye was able to maintain a good three-and-a-half to four knots.

That was an exhausting drill that would be repeated for several more hours at fifteen-to-twenty-minute intervals, which was the time between rogue waves formed by crest-on-crest wave patterns. Every rogue wave seemed to turn the dinghy turtle and swamp it. I used some of those occasions to navigate and confirm my position before rerighting the dinghy and sailing on.

The familiar blinking light on the whistle buoy two miles off Allen Harbor in Harwich Port was dimly visible on the horizon some four miles distant. My destination was in sight! My odyssey almost over! This had been a long day and night. I was ready for a rest and a joyful reunion with my family at our cottage in Harwich Port. The only remaining hurdle was the fish trap located near the whistle buoy. The fish trap areas are clearly marked on the chart, and I had sailed around this one many times but never at night. There were no lights or sound signals of any kind on the trap itself to warn of its presence. I knew that as long as I gave it a wide berth I would clear it handily. I maintained a heading to the whistle buoy that kept me out of the fish trap area as marked on the chart, knowing that the trap would not extend into the navigation channel.

Seas had grown to about eight feet in height from trough to crest, the wind between twenty and twenty-five knots in gusts. The dinghy was like a troubled teen requiring constant bailing out of jams. Again, hand over hand, I pulled in the swamped little craft, dumped the water, and released the dinghy back into the invisible maelstrom. There, it heroically fended off the relentless pounding ultimately to be forced, once again, beneath the waves by a bully sea, and dragging the Bull's Eye, ever again, to a snail's pace. My arms were weak from the repeated effort of hauling the little boat in and dumping the water out. With the whistle buoy only about two miles ahead, I surfed freely along before the wind in the wild, dark sea for a few glorious minutes, waiting for the inevitable tug of a swamped dinghy to spoil the ride. The next tug never came.

In the dim green glow of my starboard running light, I saw a tall, upright, tapered wooden pole, stripped of its bark and glistening with water, leaning toward me against my direction of travel. I noted the presence of knots where limbs had been trimmed off—all this focus on irrelevant detail to feed my denial of the horror into which I was careening. The pole was obviously stuck in the sandy bottom twenty to thirty feet below. As the pole passed to starboard, in what seemed like slow motion, I began to accept the reality that I was sailing into the fishing weir. The pole was one of dozens of such poles at 100-to-150-foot intervals supporting a three-fourth-mile-long overhead cable. The cable formed a large oval about the size and shape of a horse racing track. From that oval-shaped cable was suspended a huge net into which fish could wander but not find their way out. Fish entered through a funnel-shaped opening in the net on the opposite side from where I was. Once inside the large oval, the fish could not find the opening at the small end of the funnel back to freedom. Inside the oval enclosure, the net rested on the ocean bottom about twenty to thirty feet below the surface. The upper edge of the net hung from the cable that was strung from pole to pole. Each pole was held in place by a single guy rope. Together, the guy ropes prevented the upper edge of the net from collapsing inward. The guy ropes extended outward, away from the net, at a forty-five-degree angle downward into the water and were anchored to pegs driven into the sea floor. Not wanting to sail headlong into the net and dismast the boat on the overhead steel cable, I threw the tiller to starboard. The boat began to spin to port just as it slammed against the unyielding net. I heard the single starboard shroud screech and then groan as it scraped along the heavy cable. The wind plastered the sail against the net folding it about the cable. The boom clamored past and under the cable with a metallic clunk. The jib flailed violently against the net. The sea that drove me into the net slammed against the hull and into my sail pinning everything hopelessly against the unforgiving net. I could see little in the inky black night. I was soaked. I could hear large fish next to me inside the net smashing into one another in their panic to escape the unseen intruder trying to get at them through the net. The boat dropped into a trough, allowing the stern to wash deeper into the net. The starboard shroud, riding against the cable, held the bow somewhat into the wind and the seas. Waiting for the seas to swamp the boat, I knew I was going to die.

The Bull's Eye rose with the next advancing wave as I stood in the cockpit somehow hanging on to the sail above me. As the boat lifted in the sea, my head was driven into the overhead cable, which then scraped down the side of my face and ear onto my shoulder. I screamed with pain expecting my collarbone to snap. The excruciating pain collapsed my knees, and I fell to the floor. As I went down, the cable followed me pressing my back ever lower until the cable bridged the cockpit from the cabin top to the aft deck. At that point I fell clear of the horrid cable. I dared not move knowing that the cable was up there somewhere in the darkness and would threaten me with every wave.

As I lay on the cockpit floor peering upward trying in vain to see the damned cable, I spotted the white form of my dinghy whizzing by above me. Faintly illuminated by my white stern light, the little boat was flying through the air, thrown by a peaking sea, over the cable and into the interior of the net. The dinghy pulled the painter tight around the wooden support pole, locking the Bull's Eye in place against the net. Now all I wanted to do was to die quickly. My situation was so hopeless. No one even knew I was out there or in trouble.

Finally, my boat settled in against the net, rising with every sea and falling into every trough. The noise of the sail flogging the cable and net was appalling. The cockpit had taken in relatively little water considering the conditions. The starboard shroud continued to hold the bow into the seas as it grated up and down along the cable. The compressive forces in the mast, caused by the cable pressing against the shroud, must have been far beyond design limits. Had the mast been stepped on deck, it surely would have punched a hole through and snapped like a toothpick. Instead, the mast was stepped on the keel and supported laterally where it passed through the deck. The mast and the shroud continued to hold.

The loose boom being thrown about by the thrashing sail and wild seas was the next immediate threat. I pulled in on the mainsheet in an attempt to secure the wayward spar. That quieted both the boom and the sail, but the sail would surely be torn to shreds by that cable before long as everything chafed up and down against the motionless cable.

I decided to take down the mainsail to get it off the cable. Moving forward to the mast enabled me to evade the cable because the shroud kept the forward half of the boat away from the cable and the net. With the stern pressed hard into the net, and the starboard shroud on the cable, the cable crossed the boat overhead at an angle from the starboard shroud, just forward of amidship, across the cockpit to the port corner of the aft deck where it meets the transom. I untied the halyard from its cleat on the mast and began to lower the sail. As the sail came down, the luff rope fed itself out of the slot in the mast as was normal. But instead of dropping into the cockpit, the sail caught the wind and spray from the side forming a big loop that began to work its way down between the hull and the net as the boat rode up and down against the net. The sail, with its new degree of freedom, having been released from the mast, became more unruly and violent than ever. The boom was also freed up by the loose sail to wreak havoc. I pulled the mainsheet in tight to hold the boom down against the deck. I was afraid the sail might wrap itself under the keel as the net kept pulling it down along the hull. I had made a terrible mistake. I had to get the sail back up. I began pulling on the luff rope, at the forward edge of the sail, where it met the boom near the gooseneck fitting that holds the boom to the mast. As the boat dropped into a trough, I could retrieve a few feet of sail from between the boat and the net. But when the boat rose again, I would lose some of what I had just retrieved. Gradually, I pulled the entire sail back into the cockpit, fed the luff rope back into its slot in the mast, and raised the sail. The sail jammed partway up. Unable to see in the darkness, I had no idea what was wrong.

"Bull's Eye Caught in a Fishing Weir"

Had it snagged the cable? After several more tugs, I was ready to give up. I sat on the port seat in complete confusion while the seas continued to toss the boat up and down and the wind howled and drove spray over and into everything. The shroud scraped incessantly against the cable. Then I felt the boom held fast against the deck and remembered that I had tied it there. I released the sheet and up went the sail to its full and proper height. I could not see the sail, so I could not tell for sure if it had gone up without a twist, but I was confident that I had kept it straight. Finding my flashlight in the cockpit, I was ready to press the on switch but hesitated. Was it worth destroying my night vision for a half hour just to check the sail? I decided not. I knew the sail was okay.

I next turned my attention to the dinghy that was inside the net. Could I get it back over the net onto my side? I think, in the back of my mind, I had already begun to formulate a desperate escape plan. The aft deck was the most dangerous area because that is where I was most exposed to the cable but that is where I would have to be in order to pull the dinghy against the wind and seas and over the net. If I pulled the boom in hard with the sheet and made the sheet fast, I could hang on to the end of the boom or the sheet itself while I wrestled with the dinghy—maybe. Slowly inching my way aft with my back arched and head down to protect myself from the cable, I still managed to get hit now and then by the unseen menace as the boat rose in the seas from every trough. My life vest offered a protective cushion against the hard steel cable each time it struck me on the back and pressed me toward the floor. I could not seem to stay clear. With the boat moving around so much in the seaway, I could not predict exactly where the cable would be at any given time.

One strike by the cable knocked me off balance and against the starboard cockpit combing. As I reached for support over the side of the boat, my entire right arm got caught, trapping me between the boat and the net. The force of the boat against the net was too great for me to free my arm. The quarter-inch hemp webbing of the net bruised and abraded my arm painfully before the boat surged away enough to release my arm. Now, I was bleeding like shark bait.

I carefully positioned myself in a sitting position on the port quarter of the aft deck and pulled the mainsheet tight for support in order to attempt to retrieve the dinghy. Satisfied that I was clear of the cable, I began to pull on the painter gathering the line in until the dinghy hit the net and stopped. I was so close to the cable each time the boat rose on a sea, that I could touch it. In fact, I could brace myself against the cable momentarily with my left hand as I pulled on the dinghy painter with my right. I had to release my grasp on the cable as the boat fell back into a trough. I did not know how I would be able to get the dinghy over the net, being unable to reach it with my arms. The white stern light gave me enough illumination to see the dinghy at eye level only a few feet away each time the Bull's Eye came up on a crest. All I needed was a rogue wave to float the dinghy over the net—if I were strong enough to pull the boat over the net and cable against the advancing wave. I waited. Every once in a while, not wanting to miss my opportunity, I pulled against a large wave only to fail by pulling the dinghy into, but not over, the cable. This too was exhausting.

Finally, the right wave came in lifting the Bull's Eye hard against the cable. I pulled with all my might. The dinghy came over onto my side of the net! As both boats settled into the following trough, the Bull's Eye began to slide along the net, no longer anchored to it by the dinghy. The very next wave threw the dinghy back over the net and re-anchored the Bull's Eye. Another exercise in futility! I knew then that if I were ever to escape the net, I would have to sacrifice the dinghy. That, I was finally prepared to do. The most significant revelation to me was how easily the Bull's Eye slid along the net when freed of its constraint. That is when I first seriously considered attempting to sail my way to freedom.

Although I had actually seen little of my overall predicament in the darkness of the night, I had a general vision in my mind of where I was and how the boat was lying against the cable and the net. Based on that vision, I theorized that if I could get up enough speed along the net and cable, I could swing the stern into the net enough to get the starboard shroud off the cable. This, in turn, might permit me to increase speed into the wind on a close reach and come about onto the starboard tack. I would then be home free. The only catch was that I would get only one chance. A failed attempt would drive me into the supporting guy rope holding the next pole, and I would be pinned again, this time with no chance of escape—or worse. And I only had about one hundred feet, or five boat lengths, to perform this maneuver before sailing into the next pole and guy rope.

I groped around in the lazarette under the aft deck for a short length of line to secure the Bull's Eye to the net in preparation for cutting the dinghy loose. With the line in hand, I moved over to the starboard side carefully avoiding the overhead cable. From a kneeling position on the aft end of the starboard seat, I discovered that I could pull the boat backward along the net by hand. I inched the boat as far back as I could toward the pole anchoring the dinghy to give myself as much running distance as possible to the next pole in front of the boat. There, within a boat length of the pole behind the boat, I used the short length of line to tie the Bull's Eye directly to the lattice of the net. Before releasing the dinghy into the wild, I untied the painter from its cleat on the aft deck and retied it to the net so that only the short length of spare line was holding the Bull's Eye in place and no longer the dinghy painter. The net held. I could release the dinghy any time or just leave it tied to the net.

I was ready. Did I really want to do this and risk getting tangled up in the next guy rope and wrecking my boat? I could just stay put until morning and wait for someone to see me and send for a rescue team. My heart began to pound. Both options were awful. I did not want to end my otherwise successful trip with an ignominious rescue, but then, I did not want to wreck my boat either. While agonizing over my options, I had carelessly centered myself in the cockpit and was struck again on the head by the damned cable. When painfully pressed to the floor once more, I became aware of the substantial amount of water taken aboard in the past few hours. The time was only 3:00 a.m. Any rescue would be hours away at best. My decision was made. I would risk a sail away.

I tried to think through and anticipate every detail of my escape. How would I know how far I was traveling along the net? I could not see the net going by nor could I see the water to use that as a guide. Yes, I could see the net going by in the glow of my green, starboard running light! That would have to suffice. Was I correct about the spacing of poles? The risks were high. Using my little green bucket, I bailed as much of the water out of the cockpit as I could, throwing it into the net. I pulled in the jib sheet for a close reach and reset the mainsheet for a close reach as well. The boat strained to move forward. The mainsail was still folded over the cable by the force of the wind while the aft end of the hull and boom crossed under the cable at an angle against the net. The aft portion of the mainsail kept riding up and down chafing heavily on the cable. The starboard shroud continued to hold the forward end of the boat out away from the cable so that only the stern lay against the net. From this condition, I was to start my run to freedom—or to disaster!

One final desperate thought: if worse came to worse and I ensnared my boat in the next pole and guy rope, and the boat swamped, maybe I could abandon the Bull's Eye and climb up onto the net. Once on the net, I could work my way back to the pole where my dinghy is tied and make my escape in the dinghy. I decided to leave the dinghy tied to the net for just that contingency.

With the boat in a trough and the cable safely high above me, I crossed over to the starboard side, my open rigging knife in hand. Feeling around for the line that held the boat to the net, I made a strong cut to release the boat. Nothing happened. I had just cut my dinghy loose! I sat there stunned by my stupidity and the loss of my only backup option. Again, I felt for the line. This time I found the right one and, with the boat dropping into another trough, cut it. I bolted to the port side and grabbed the tiller. The Bull's Eye was already moving and picking up speed. I centered the tiller pulling it slightly to port to force the stern away from the net. The starboard shroud scraped agonizingly along the cable but kept the hull away from the net. Aligning the boat parallel to the net would maximize its speed. Within a few boat lengths, I had reached what I estimated to be full speed for the boat under those conditions. I could feel that the boat was no longer accelerating. I pushed the tiller hard to starboard. The stern swung into the net. The starboard shroud came off the cable. I noted the heading on the compass and held it. The boat left the net and cable behind, and picked up speed on a close reach. Having no idea how close I was to the next pole and guy rope, I again pushed the tiller hard to leeward to begin a rotation onto the starboard tack. The sails began to luff as the Bull's Eye turned into the wind. The boat slowed in the huge seas but kept rotating to port. Then I felt the sails fill on the starboard tack. I was over! I never saw a pole or guy rope and have no idea how close I came to them but did not care—and I still don't care! I was free! I cried without restraint in the privacy of the dark sea, sobbing uncontrollably as much from exhaustion as from relief as I sailed away from that hellish net.

Ten or fifteen minutes distanced me from the fishing weir by at least half a mile. Feeling safely positioned in open, deep water, I heaved to and fell asleep on the floor of the cockpit.

I awakened to bright sunlight. Looking up over the cockpit combing, I could see the fishing weir about a half mile distant. The time was 5:30 a.m. I had hardly moved at all in the past two and a half hours. The sun was just above the horizon but was already casting a warm light. Dragging myself up onto a seat, I became aware of my injuries. My head and right arm were very sore, my back hurt, and my collarbone was killing me, but I was a happy camper nonetheless. I was weary and hungry, but Allen Harbor was in sight. I reset sail toward the harbor. As I passed the weir, I noticed that it extended well into the navigation channel. I confirmed that observation with some hockey puck bearings to visible land marks. No wonder I hit it. Would anyone move it? Not a chance. They would remark the charts first. The wind and seas of the night had disappeared, morphing into gentle, user-friendly waves to usher me into home port.

Sailing past the breakwater into Allen Harbor was a pure joy. Once in the little harbor, I found the empty mooring reserved for me by my father. However, without a dinghy, I sailed past the mooring to the dock where I made a safe and easy landing. As I approached the dock upwind, I jumped off with a bow line in my hand and secured it to the nearest cleat. Then I jumped quickly back aboard to drop the main before its sheet got tangled up in the tiller allowing the sail to catch the wind and drive the boat against the dock. I rigged a stern line and one spring. I grabbed my boat bag out of the cuddy cabin and headed across the parking lot to the street.

About a mile and a half brought me to Ginger Plumb Lane, a sandy, dead-end road connecting the main drag to the beach. Along that road was my parents' cottage. I walked into the house and called out, "Hello, Mom. I'm here."

She came running into the kitchen, saw me, and ran to me almost yelling, "I'm so glad to see you! We were so worried about you! How was your trip?"

"Great!"

CHAPTER VIII

KEY WEST TO
THE DRY TORTUGAS

During the early years, the late 1960s and 1970s, Roy Debski was a frequent sailing companion in my Bull's Eye. Smitten by the lure of adventure sailing, he purchased a fifteen-foot Marshal catboat, later upgrading to an eighteen-footer. While still sailing the smaller boat, Roy was transferred from East Hartford, Connecticut, to West Palm Beach, Florida, by his employer, Pratt & Whitney Aircraft. He took his boat with him. Whereas, a catboat is a familiar sight in New England where the design was first used off Cape Cod by commercial fishermen to tend crab and lobster pots in shallow coastal waters, in West Palm, the catboat was unique, to say the least, and drew considerable attention wherever it went.

The fiberglass Marshal cats are also unique among catboats. They are among the few, if not the only ones, that have been modified to take advantage of lightweight aluminum spars. Traditional wooden cats have full bow cheeks to support the heavy wooden masts located as far forward as possible. Those full bow cheeks render the boats ponderous to windward and slower than a sloop on most other points of sail. Most modern fiberglass catboats are produced from molds formed around carefully sanded and smoothed wooden hulls and, consequently, carry the same full cheek designs as their wooden forebears with all of their attendant performance deficits. The Marshal designs have been trimmed down with slightly hollow bow cheeks for a cleaner entry resulting in fast boats that can point as well to windward as many sloops. Roy's eighteen-foot Marshal cat was a joy to sail.

Like most (maybe all) catboats, tiller forces were strong requiring well-developed biceps for long hauls. Catboat rigging philosophies are different from most other sailboat designs. For example, full sail on a modern catboat is equivalent to the full main and Genoa jib on a sloop. A single reef in the catboat mainsail is equivalent to full working sails on a sloop. And to "reef" a catboat, a double reef is required. The generous beam of a catboat lends itself to roomy accommodations for two in the cabin. The cockpit is also quite spacious. Although this design makes for comfortable sailing, it is a potential swamping liability in heavy seas.

The sailing characteristics of a shallow draft catboat are very different from those of a deep-keeled sloop. One of the most important differences is in comparative stiffness. The sloop will stiffen (increase its righting moment) as its angle of heel increases. The heavy weight on the end of the deep keel on a sloop increases the righting moment as the boat heels by moving farther and farther off center.[2] Oh brother, I see eyes glazing over. Hang in there; this geeky, techy stuff for the "serious types" only lasts for a few paragraphs, then we're back to the good stuff which, by the way, gets really good. Continuing: A catboat's righting moment, on the other hand, increases at first, then decreases suddenly and sharply as the boat continues to increase its angle of heel. This happens because the internal ballast of the catboat—five hundred pounds of lead ingots in Roy's boat—is on a short moment arm, which exerts a minimal (and suddenly decreasing) righting moment on the boat.[3] The practical consequence of this is that a catboat is easily overturned if not carefully tended in high or gusty winds. The initial stiffness of the catboat can give the skipper a false sense of stability at greater angles of heel.

Another potential hazard in a catboat is its strong tendency to weather vane into the wind, the cause of the strong tiller forces on all points of sail. This characteristic manifests itself most disturbingly in a following sea and can easily end in a broached and/or swamped boat as one unnamed skipper discovered with his wife aboard in Jupiter Inlet—a notorious breaking inlet from the open sea into Florida's Lake Worth. As the boat's stern begins to lift to a quartering wave, both the wave and the force in the mainsheet strive to twist the boat broadside to the advancing sea. If, at (or, preferably, prior to) that critical moment, the tiller is not pulled sharply to windward to align the boat stern-to the wave, the boat will broach, that is, spin uncontrollably to windward until broadside to the breaking wave, and if the wave is big enough, the catboat will be rolled completely over and swamped. The only recourse at that point is to retrieve the boat after it washes up—dismasted—onto the beach. If broached in the open sea, the boat will be lost.

By April 1982, I was well versed in the sailing of catboats, both Roy's and my father's eighteen-foot Cape Cod catboat. Over a period of years, Roy and I had sailed in one or the other of his two Marshal cats the entire length of Florida's east coast from Cape Canaveral to Key West. We were ready for the push to the Dry Tortugas. The only thing we really needed was a stable weather pattern so that we would not get caught in an open and stormy sea. April of that year was looking very good with no tropical developments forecast for the foreseeable future.

We trailered the boat to the western end of Key West where we launched it at a ramp in the area of Key West Bight. Stepping the heavy and cumbersome aluminum mast—but still lighter than its solid wood counterpart—was a struggle made possible only by the nifty homemade rigging crane that Roy had built for that purpose. After provisioning for about ten days, we set out early the next day sailing south then southwest into West Channel and finally westward then northwestward in a big lazy loop toward the Marquesas Keys some twenty nautical miles due west of Key West. On our way we passed several small keys to our north including Crawfish, Man, Woman, and Boca Grande Keys. The weather was warm and sunny with a fair breeze that whisked us on our way.

Arriving shortly after noon, we entered Boca Grande Channel on our northwest approach to the uninhabited ring of keys called Marquesas. I wanted to stay the night inside that protective ring so as not to be anchored in open water all night. We slowly made our way toward the deepest of two navigable entrances to the lagoon. The rise and fall of the tide was less than two feet, but in an area where the water is only a few feet deep, that can be critical. The tide was low during our approach, which made grounding all but inevitable. The first rattle of the centerboard inside its trunk (housing) came a good mile off the ring of mangrove trees emanating from the barely dry sandy keys forming the atoll. We raised the centerboard slightly and continued on. Again, the rattle of the board in the trunk, this time accompanied by a slowing of the boat. Again, we raised the board to clear the sandy bottom, each time increasing our sideslip. Finally, with almost no centerboard exposed below the boats bottom, and the boat side-slipping like a leaf on the water, the time had come to get out and pull.

If we could only go another few hundred yards, the water color indicated a deepening at the entrance to the atoll. I donned a pair of midcalf rubber boots to protect from the assortment of stinging sea creatures that littered the sea floor. Of particular concern were the purple, spiny sea urchins that seemed to be everywhere. Although over eighty degrees Fahrenheit, the water felt refreshingly cool under the intense tropical sun. The boots filled with water as I lowered myself into the water, which barely wet my bathing suit. With my weight now out of the boat, and with a draft of only about twenty-one inches with the centerboard fully raised, the catboat floated freely in the shallow water. Roy handed me the anchor line, which I extended to about twelve feet for comfortable towing, as he settled back into the steering seat to keep the boat well pointed while I tugged and towed. I will have to admit that Roy was most helpful in keeping me motivated by hurling instructions and insults as fast as he could think of them.

Keeping my eyes ahead and focused on the sea floor where I was about to step next, I noticed a slightly raised mound of sand directly in my path. I stopped. Nothing moved, so I advanced very slowly. Suddenly, a stingray darted from its protective covering and vanished in a cloud of sand. The rubber boots would have offered little, if any, protection had I stepped on that "mound of sand."

All was going quite well until the boat began to drag the bottom ever so slightly. Even that gentle contact increased my effort to keep the boat moving. Roy moved forward to even the trim, which helped to reduce the contact with the sea floor. We were so close to the deeper water, I had to make it! I dug my heels into the hardpacked sand and pulled heavily on the anchor line to maintain a forward momentum.

Mistake—major mistake!

My heels broke through the hard, thin crust on which I had been walking for over half an hour. The feeling of sand pouring into my boots and locking them to my feet, coupled with the awareness of sinking into the soft sand below the crust and the feeling of cool water rising up over my genitals, my navel and up my chest toward my face with no sense of bottom beneath my feet sent a paralyzing panic surging through my tortured brain. My heart pounded out adrenaline into every extremity of my body. Was I to die out here in quicksand with not a trace? I could not move my feet. "Don't let go of the anchor line!" I silently screamed at myself. I gulped air and dropped below the surface struggling to free my feet. Incredibly, they moved. Semireclined and hanging on to the adjacent crust of the sea floor, I kicked my feet free. I raised my feet above my head to let the sand pour out of my boots. Then I scrambled up onto the unbroken crust and stood up, rope in hand in the knee-deep water, heart pounding, breathing like a marathon runner, and stared up at Roy, who stared back down at me as much in shock at the spectacle he had just witnessed as I.

Now what? All manner of thoughts raced through my head. One of the first was astonishment at the light weight nature of the "sand." It was not sand at all, but finely ground coral, which is why I had been able to free myself so easily from its grasp. Had that been real silica sand, the outcome might have been quite different. But let's not dwell on that. Here we were with me standing on a reef only a few hundred feet from our destination and unable to move in any direction without continuing our march across the sand. Actually, with the anchor line in my fist, I always had a self-rescue of last resort in my grasp. And Roy could always have helped drag me up and out of the sand from the safety of the boat. But I did not need any of that. I had gotten myself out of the sand without any assistance. Hell, that sand wasn't so bad after all! Let's keep going!

Line in hand, I walked carefully around the hole I had just made in the sea floor, and continued on our merry way toward the entrance of the lagoon in the atoll. I broke through the fragile crust and fell into the soft sand twice more before reaching deeper water, each time rescuing myself as I did the first time but without the extreme angst. As I walked and pulled, I had time to reflect and recall, among other things, the chart. Yes, the chart, which in large bold letters spelled out the name of the larger reef that supported the atoll into which we were headed: "THE QUICKSANDS." Oh, but what's in a name?

At last, in deeper water, we partially lowered the centerboard and sailed through the narrow inlet into the lagoon. What a paradise! A beautiful shining sea about two miles across completely surrounded by mangrove trees jutting out from barely visible sand (coral) keys. We anchored in "deep" water that might even have been over our heads. Able to relax for a while, we discussed the day's adventure. Much luck was with us.

For instance, I never came in contact with a spiny sea urchin during my thrashing about in the quicksand. That alone could have spoiled my day. A few inches less of water depth could have stranded us hopelessly on the reef until the tide came in (up) forcing us to "feel" our way into the lagoon after dark. I, to this day, have no idea how deep the quicksand is out there since I never touched hard bottom. Suddenly we were hungry—really hungry—not having eaten since morning.

Roy broke out a large can of Dinty Moore beef stew and a bottle of red wine. It just doesn't get any better than that! Out came our best silver (stainless steel), Melmac plates, and cups. Paradise deserves nothing less.

On empty stomachs, the wine quickly warmed the cockles of our hearts. Conversation became animated and lively, language spicy and fun. Paradise was now. We ate, we drank, we talked, we laughed, and we peed over the side. We had conquered the world. Basically, we were decompressing from a stressful and scary day. But the day was not over—not nearly over!

Exhausted and relaxed, we sat in the cockpit of the boat and drank in the luxurious warmth of the fading tropical sun. A motorboat wake appeared several hundred yards distant and ran across the lagoon. Problem was, there was no motorboat. A large fish, probably a shark, was swimming at high speed just below the surface in the shallow water, possibly trapped in the lagoon and frantically looking for a way out. Not attaching any particular significance to this at the time, we knew that swimming in the lagoon was not an option.

Conversation gradually subsided, and we sat there, for the most part, just thinking while watching the sun go down.

Roy broke the silence. "I hear a ringing in my ears."

Stunned, I replied, "I hear it too."

We sat there looking at each other and around us. I began to sweat. The noise was getting louder, but we could see nothing. Finally, I went below and began to put on my long cotton pants over my bathing suit. Roy stayed in the cockpit. I had slipped one leg into my pants and was putting the second leg in when the boat suddenly started to rock violently. I heard yelling and bodies slamming around in the cockpit. Roy was being attacked and was fighting somebody off. I had to assist him. But I had to get my pants on first. As I finished hastily buckling my belt, I lunged at the open companionway but froze dead in my tracks. The opening darkened with a cloud of insects that smelled my presence and swarmed into the cabin to eat me alive! Tiny mosquitoes covered me instantly from head to toe. They must have smelled our presence from the mangroves around the edge of the lagoon and waited for the setting sun to swarm and dine. As I breathed in to scream, they filled my mouth and nose. I coughed and choked and spat. I chewed some of them up and spat them out. They invaded my throat and sinuses and burned my nasal passages. They got caught between my eyes and eyelids. I had to keep my eyes shut. They were in my ears. They covered my naked back, chest, and arms and stung me everywhere even as they became trapped in my armpits. I panicked and flung myself against everything trying to squish them against anything I could. I only managed to hurt myself more. I grabbed my handkerchief and breathed into it to keep the little invaders out of my lungs. My instinct was to jump into the ocean, but the thought of the shark prevented that move.

From the cockpit, I heard Roy yelling, "Get the Cutter (insect repellent)!" I grabbed the spray can and covered myself. Then I threw the can up to Roy who sprayed himself. The biting mostly stopped, but the insects did not leave. Roy had the good sense to load a Cutter mosquito punk aboard, which he dragged out of hiding and lit. The punk burned like a slow fuse, releasing a sweet-smelling smoke into the cabin, which drove the little devils out for good. We then covered the companionway opening with a screen and began the slow and deliberate process of killing the remaining insects now trapped below with us. The itching was barely tolerable. However, we knew not to scratch the bites and create infection sites. So we grinned and bore it until the itching stopped a few hours later. In the meantime, we busied ourselves cleaning the mess. The inside of the cabin was greasy with smeared insect bodies. We cleaned and cleaned trying to ignore the infernal itching. We let the punk burn for almost an hour. When the itching stopped, we both fell asleep on our bunks and never awoke until morning.

We awakened about 6:00 a.m. to the sharp tugging of the boat at its anchor. A gusty breeze was tossing the boat to and fro. Peering up out of the companionway hatch, I could see a thunderstorm forming about two miles distant. I took a bearing on the center of the storm and repeated that measurement every five minutes. The building storm was not headed our way but could intersect our path as we headed out for the Tortugas. Based on its slow speed, I figured that we could easily keep ahead of it if we left immediately. We weighed anchor and headed for the south entrance of the lagoon under the power of our little outboard engine. The tide was high, making for an easy exit into deeper water. Once clear of the atoll and well into the Straits of Florida, we set sail and headed west. As we made our turn, the storm was centered about a mile and a half to the southeast of us. In that short amount of time, the storm had built significantly and was looking very black and angry but was surrounded by bright blue sky.

The storm began to overtake us slowly. The center was dark with rain. The periphery was alive with swirling clouds that dipped downward in conical swirls bobbing up and down as they grew and shrunk back like living, breathing stalactites. The storm had closed to within about a mile of us. Wind was light but fitful and gusty. One of the swirling cones grew quite long, reaching halfway to the water, and then dropped all the way down instantly raising a white froth around its dark center. A full-blown water spout was born, its snakelike form writhing menacingly as its frothy bottom danced about its relatively fixed upper source point. I altered course slightly to put the storm directly astern. The water spout lasted about ten or fifteen minutes then vanished. Five minutes later, a second spout dropped then a third. Both lasted between five and ten minutes each before evaporating into thin air. As the sun rose higher in the sky, the storm began to subside and shrink in both size and ferocity. In little more than an hour, no sign of it remained, and we were once again surrounded by clear air and warm sunshine—an amazing spectacle indeed.

We were quite happy to leave the Marquesas behind. The goal now was to not miss our small target some fifty nautical miles to our west. With a daytime view to the horizon of only six to seven miles from the deck of our boat, we could not afford to be off course much at all. However, at night, the 150-foot tall light house on Loggerhead Key in the Dry Tortugas would be visible for at least twenty nautical miles in any direction, giving us much more margin for error. In addition, other lighted markers along the way would be visible for several miles at night whereas those same markers in daylight would be very hard to spot at any more than a mile distant. With all that in mind, we had timed our departure from the Marquesas to arrive in the Tortugas near or after dark on our second day out. From the Marquesas, we would sail all day and all night in open water and make landfall in the Tortugas near the end of the second day. The weather was perfect, and we were on our way.

We were soon completely out of sight of land. As the hours passed, fear grew knowing how exposed we were in that open water in our little boat. We were heading toward the open Atlantic hoping to see a very small target before passing it by. What if we wandered too far off course and never saw it? The longer we sailed, the larger the ocean seemed. We had to keep our imaginations in check. The only possibility of sending a distress signal of any kind was with our primitive EPIRB (Emergency Position Indicating Radio Beacon), a far cry from modern

EPIRBs that can send out emergency signals to satellite systems that include not only a precise longitude and latitude of your position but a description of your boat, cell phone number, VHF identification, and other pertinent data. Our EPIRB could only send out a weak distress signal on 121.5 MHz in the hope that a passing airliner would hear it and respond. But we had sufficient diversions to keep our minds occupied with less serious concerns. As mealtimes approached, Roy would prepare amazingly good breakfasts, lunches, and dinners. We suffered not for lack of adequate food and nutrition.

Not far from the Marquesas, we spotted an interesting activity in the water ahead. What appeared to be a huge egg floating on end in the water had two heads and was unnervingly active. Closer inspection revealed a seam around the "egg." The "egg" turned out to be two loggerhead turtles mating. Their shells are not flat on the underside but somewhat wavy shaped. Where the male shell goes in, the female shell goes out so that when they mate, they fit together perfectly. The two turtles had their flippers wrapped around each other and were flapping them enthusiastically on each other's back. We sailed silently to within about twenty-five yards of the pair before they broke apart, swam around our boat, and left the scene.

Although we had not seen a single boat all day, as the sun began to set, we began to set our running lights in preparation for the long night ahead. This was quite a ritual that took all of a half hour to complete. While I manned the tiller, Roy dug out the three running lights. Lining them up in the cockpit, he methodically filled each one with kerosene, adjusted the wicks, and lit each one with a match. Each lamp consisted of a large glass Fresnel lens in a brass housing about eight inches high. Once lit, the lamps were hooked into place on each side of the cabin and on the stern. They were so well designed that they could be mostly submerged for hours at a time without going out. When the lamps were finally lighted and in place, they left three trails of smoke over one hundred feet long behind the boat. The scene was picturesque to say the least and reminiscent of days long gone by.

The first night passed without incident. Roy and I took turns at the tiller. We did not have a structured schedule but changed watches as our bodies dictated. When off watch, we would sleep until we awoke naturally. When the tiller man got tired, the watch would change and he could sleep. This worked quite well and kept us from both fading out at the same time. We used this approach to watches for night and day sailing. At night, one of us would always be sleeping. That enabled us to be awake together during most of the day for meals and other activities. Daytime naps were generally short. Although a little loosey-goosey, this watch "schedule" allowed us both more than enough sleep time. We had used similar watches successfully for multiday sails on previous trips.

The following day was very long indeed and filled with the anxiety of being heavily committed to the open sea with no land in sight and an increasingly long way back. We began searching the horizon with binoculars for any sign of a buoy or land-based beacon. Nothing—for hours—nothing but the clear horizon loomed in every direction. We did not even see any boats. I began thinking about the possibility of not seeing anything ever. At what point would we reverse course and head back to Florida? In my own mind, I had decided that we would sail the night, and if no sighting were made by sunrise, we would turn back. Such a decision would, of course, have to be discussed with Roy, but I did not want to panic him by revealing my sudden insecurity and lack of confidence in my own navigational skills. He was trusting me to get him to the Tortugas safely, and I had given him every assurance that I could even though I had never ventured that far before on dead reckoning alone, which he knew. Yet on a more rational note, we had maintained good compass discipline the entire time, so I had no valid reason to question our position. I just had to keep my cool, trust the compass, and press on. Then, finally, after what seemed to me like eternity, we saw our first mark—a mere speck a few points off the starboard bow. Sailing up to it to make a positive identification, we had located the east side of Southeast Channel into the Tortugas with several hours of daylight remaining. Our navigation had been right on the money! Rarely have I ever felt such relief in my entire life as I did at that moment! We would not die at sea, at least not that day, and I had not slobbered my insecurities all over Roy's image of me. Once again, I renewed my confidence in the old adage, "Trust your instruments, not your gut."

We followed the deep water channel around Bush Key and into the anchorage at Garden Key, our final destination and home of the famous Fort Jefferson (more about that later). We dropped anchor before dark and slept the night away.

The morning again greeted us with bright sunshine. After our usual breakfast of cereal and cold milk with raisins and bananas, orange juice, and hot coffee; we weighed anchor, motored to the dock, and went ashore. We landed near the entrance to Fort Jefferson, a huge brick structure that covers almost the entire land mass of Garden Key. We were greeted by uniformed National Park Service rangers who graciously offered us a tour of the fort, for the usual fee, of course. We eagerly accepted. Several of the rangers were intrigued by the manner in which we had arrived at that remote outpost. We happily shared our story with them, but our attentions were soon diverted, captured by the undeniable sights, smells and haunting echoes that reverberated with the history of human struggle to survive that hostile bastion.

What secrets hide within the eight-foot thick, moldy brick walls of this massive fortress sprawling in the Dry Tortugas? The fort's two thousand perfectly matched archways stretch endlessly into shadows, some hiding cannon, others designed to look as if firepower were hiding inside. The deep, seventy-foot wide mote surrounding the entire fort mirrors the fifty-foot high, red brick walls, conjuring up images of medieval castles.

During the late Middle Ages, Spanish adventurers skirted the Florida coast on their way to claim treasures hidden in the hills of Mexico. Ponce de Leon was among those who anchored off these coral islands and named them "las Tortugas" (the Turtles) after the hundreds of nesting sea turtles he had seen. Later, other early mariners renamed them the Dry Tortugas because of the lack of fresh water.

Despite the absence of drinking water, the Dry Tortugas, with its natural anchorage between coral reefs, offered ships protection from the fury of the seas. From the time of Ponce de Leon to the early 1820s, pirates sought refuge in the Tortugas, a vantage point from which to ambush marine commerce traveling from Europe to the port of New Orleans.

American naval activities increased around the Tortugas as battles were fought to eradicate the pirates. From these experiences, the U.S. military realized the importance of the island chain's location in relationship to key American shipping lanes. Congress, nervous over the gathering storm clouds in Europe and rumbles of unrest in nearby Spanish-held Cuba, did not want a repeat of the War of 1812. Funds were appropriated in the late 1820s to build the garrison, and work began on the $3.5 million fortress named for President Thomas Jefferson in the fall of 1846.

Unfortunately, Army surveyors selected a spoil of sand and coral boulders, so that before the fort was half built, its concrete and brick walls started to settle and crumble. And, the development of the new rifled cannon, a weapon that concentrated firepower into a tight pattern, made the fort's scatter-shot Rodman cannon and Parrott rifles, already installed and encased in concrete, virtually useless. Ten years before construction finally ground to a halt in 1875, America's greatest 19th century coastal fort was outdated. Only a handful of its 450 cannon ever fired a shot. And most of the time, the officer's and enlisted men's quarters, with their silver doorknobs and cypress walls, were home for only a fraction of the 1,500 soldiers the fort could have housed.

Occupied by Union soldiers during the Civil War, only a few warning shots were ever fired at Rebel ships. The fort that was to have saved the vulnerable Gulf coast from invasion became a prison. Then, in World War I, it functioned as a wireless radio station, later a coaling stop, and, today, it is an attraction to which as many as 18,000 scuba divers, boaters and tourists travel by plane and boat.

Fire and scavengers have ravaged much of the fort's living areas, but the two water storage systems, designed by Army General J.G. Totten more than 100 years ago, still serve the needs of National Park Service rangers who stand guard over the solitary outpost. With its hexagonal design, six symmetrical towers, and graceful support arches, Fort Jefferson is architecturally beautiful. Hundreds of New England bricklayers helped slaves and prisoners place the 40 million bricks used to build the mammoth structure, which is a half mile in perimeter. Mustard yellow bricks from north Florida and southern Georgia rise from the mean water line to about midway, where red Yankee bricks placed after the start of the Civil War reach skyward. Giant 200- and 300-pound granite boulders along with stone cutters were imported from Maine to the remote island where, for almost a year, they worked with slaves to create the elegant entrance that lies just beyond the drawbridge over the mote.

Perhaps Fort Jefferson's greatest historical significance stems not from its military record, but from its life as a prison. Samuel A. Mudd, a Maryland physician who unwittingly mended the broken leg of President Lincoln's assassin, John Wilkes Booth, was convicted in the conspiracy and sentenced to life imprisonment here. During a yellow fever outbreak in 1865, Mudd worked 24 hours a day tending the dying inmates and military at the fort. His lifesaving efforts earned him the sympathy of the entire country and, more importantly, a presidential pardon in 1869.

Weathered by hurricanes and winter northeasters, stripped by vandals of much of its armament and décor, Fort Jefferson has survived the odds to become America's Rock of Gibraltar. And, like Gibraltar, its sense of impregnability holds it aloof.[4]

Needless to say, we thoroughly enjoyed our tour of this fascinating archaeological treasure.

The following day was designated for exploring. We had to get a closer look at the 150-foot tall "skyscraper" lighthouse on Loggerhead Key only two miles west of Fort Jefferson. We set sail shortly after breakfast and headed west. Arriving at a dock with two Coast Guard boats tied up to it, we were almost immediately put upon by two young men in civvies who ran to intercept us. One might have thought that we had discovered two marooned and shipwrecked sailors who sincerely believed that they would never see civilization again. As we tied up, we listened to a frantic tail of indifference and neglect by their mates at the station on Key West. It seemed that the three young men on the island—two of which were standing before us while the third was working on the generators for the lighthouse—had run out of beer two weeks ago and clean clothes a week before that. Even food was in short supply. They claimed to have radioed the CG station on Key West many times to send relief supplies but to no avail. Their two boats were both inoperative for lack of simple spare parts, so the boys could not fetch their own supplies. How effective was our gallant CG in the Dry Tortugas when our potential rescuers themselves needed to be rescued? Anyway, we could at least help them with one of their problems, the laundry. They asked us if we could ferry them to Garden Key to do their laundry in the facility provided for the National Park Service personnel at Fort Jefferson. We agreed, and they ran back to the lighthouse to retrieve the laundry.

Well now, try to imagine, if you will, the size of a pile of laundry generated by three active young men over a three-week period of time—not pretty! Now try to imagine that pile of laundry in the cockpit of our little eighteen-foot catboat with nary an inch of clearance from the top of the pile to the bottom of the boom. Now add the two young Coast Guardsmen, Roy and me, and you have the setting for an exciting episode of the Keystone Cops. And that, my dear reader, is exactly how we ferried our desperate charges to Garden Key, the land of Laundromats and beer. Several hours later, the ferry service departed once again back to Loggerhead Key, this time laden with a happier, cleaner, and more fragrant pile of lads and clothing.

Not yet ready to leave this tropical paradise, we needed yet another day to explore the reefs. We sailed out a short distance from Garden Key and dropped the hook. Donning snorkel gear and swim fins, over the side we went. Swimming along the surface, I could see the bottom littered with little more than purple, spiny sea urchins. I drew a breath and dove about five feet in the ten-to-twelve-foot deep water. I was at once surrounded by a school of sunfish about a foot long. I stopped and looked as they looked back at me. Suddenly they all scattered, some to the left and some to the right, all that is, except for one directly in front of my face mask. I moved toward it; it moved back. I moved back; it moved toward me. I stopped; it stopped. I let myself rise slowly to the surface to breathe. As I did so, the fish turned sideways revealing the four foot form of a barracuda. How much it looked like one of the small sunfish head-on! Off it went. At the surface, I scanned the area for any sign of the deadly man-of-war jellyfish—nothing. Roy had seen the barracuda approach the school but had no way to warn me not that I could have done anything about it anyway.

The bottom became quite hilly as we swam, the depth varying from as much as twenty feet to as little as three feet. Approaching the crest of a hill that rose to within only a few feet of the surface, we had to proceed very carefully to avoid scraping any of the dozens of spiny urchins sitting on the sand. With my focus on the hilltop, I did not see what lay below in the valley beyond. There, in a depression some twenty feet below the surface, and just above the sand, lay a large brown shark basking in the sun. The shark was surrounded by five or six other smaller fish, one of which I recognized as a grouper. The others may have been bass and snappers. They all looked like different species. Roy and I stopped as soon as we saw them. The shark, somewhat annoyed at being disturbed, slowly turned away and left, taking his entourage with him.

Feeling like we were rapidly using up our good luck chits, Roy and I decided to return to the boat and continue our sightseeing from a safer vantage.

The time to head home had arrived. The next day, with stores of water, food, and ice replenished, we weighed anchor for the last time in the Dry Tortugas and set sail for Key West, this time bypassing the Marquesas. The weather continued to cooperate, but as we pulled into Key West Bight two days later, we began hearing forecasts of an approaching weather front. By that time the forecast was of little interest to us since we would soon be on the road north in his car with our trusty little home-away-from-home trailing dutifully behind us.

CHAPTER IX

YVALEDON

My current boat, *Yvaledon*, is an eighteen-foot Herreshoff sloop built by the Cape Cod Shipbuilding Co. and classified as a Goldeneye. The underbody design is essentially identical to that of the Bull's Eye—that is, a wineglass hull form with a cast lead weight equal to slightly more than half the total weight of the boat and located at the bottom of a deep keel for stability. The lower surface of the lead runs along the very bottom of the keel and most of the way up the stem (the foremost edge of the boat) toward the waterline thus offering substantial protection to the fiberglass in the event of a grounding. Although this hull form results in a slower boat incapable of planing, it offers a seaworthy and sea-kindly (comfortable) boat free of pounding and shuddering in a seaway, characteristics that are highly desirable for long distance, all-weather sailing. With the rudder safely hidden behind the keel, there is little risk of the rudder being broken off and no risk of the rudder getting hung up on unseen lobster pot buoys, especially at night. And with the rudder extending to the very bottom of the keel, there is no loss of steering control from the rudder lifting out of the water in choppy seas as often happens with short spade rudders. Above the waterline, the two boats begin to differ.

The Goldeneye hull has short overhangs above the waterline, meaning that, the deck length is not much greater than the waterline length. The Bull's Eye, by comparison, has long overhangs that cause it to hobbyhorse (pitch) somewhat in a seaway. Other than that, the two designs behave very much alike in all sea conditions. Both boats are always controllable and predictable even under the most extreme conditions.

The sail plans of the two boats are radically different. This paragraph is a little on the technical side, but is still a fun read, and will be of particular interest to the sailor who may be considering giving adventure sailing a try. The Bull's Eye has a short rig (short mast) with a large mainsail and a tiny jib. The center-of-effort of the main is so far aft of the center-of-lateral plane of the hull that the boat cannot be sailed to windward with the main alone. Huh? Do I see those eyes glazing over again? Come on back; it's really not as complicated as it sounds. Let's take another tack, if you will. If you pushed against the mainsail with a stick at a point that produced the same affect on the boat as the wind pushing evenly on the whole sail, you would be pushing at the center-of-effort. Now, that wasn't so bad, was it? The only difference between the stick and the wind is that the wind won't poke a hole in your sail. The center-of-lateral plane is the same thing on the hull. If you pushed on the hull with a stick at a point where the boat would move sideways through the water without twisting to one side or the other, or up or down, you would be pushing at the center-of-lateral plane. The Bull's Eye's center-of-effort of the mainsail is so far aft of the center-of-lateral plane of the hull that, without the jib, the wind forces the boat to weathervane into the wind and the rudder is not able to fully counteract that twisting force. Thus the jib, small as it is, is essential to balance the boat so that it can be sailed to windward. In addition to the standard, or working, jib, my Bull's Eye was equipped with a larger Genoa jib, often referred to as the Jenny, to provide more go-power in light air (gentle breezes). The larger Genoa jib also balanced the boat. But because of its size, most of the Genoa overlapped the main in such a manner that the overall balance of the combined main and Genoa was exactly the same as the balance of the combined main and working jib. Since the small working jib on the Bull's Eye flies entirely forward of the mast, it has a club (short, curved boom) that enables the jib to tack itself from side to side when changing from port to starboard tack and back. This frees the sailor to tack without tending a jib sheet (the line used to let the sail in or out, as needed, to best catch the wind), a major convenience that, in my opinion, more than compensates for not being able to sail with the main only.

The Goldeneye, on the other hand, has a very tall rig and an oak bowsprit that juts forward of the boat's bow (over the water) to extend the sail area equal to that of a twenty-foot boat. The Goldeneye is a fast, powerful little yacht and can be easily sailed to windward under the main alone. Despite these differences, both boats are perfectly balanced (fully rigged with main and jib) with light tiller forces on all points of sail.

Oh, by the way, *Yvaledon* is an acronym for Yvette, Valerie, Eddy, and Donna, my four great kids.

BEFORE WE SAILED

A boat had to be built. *Riding the Wild Ocean*, the story, actually began for *Yvaledon* in 2005. Features were added to the standard Goldeneye specifically to improve its safety and comfort for all weather, offshore, and for day and night sailing. The Goodwins of Cape Cod Shipbuilding (CCS) were wonderful in helping me to configure my boat for its intended hazardous duty. In this section, I will explain exactly what those special features are and why I incorporated them. The casual reader may elect to skip this section unless, of course, you feel compelled to further subject yourself to my indefatigable wit.

PREPARING THE BOAT

First, a word about critical construction features that are standard in CCS boats, making them particularly well suited for heavy-duty use. The hull and deck are both constructed with fiber glass cloth (not matte) into which epoxy is manually forced by a labor-intensive process that yields a form of superior strength and stiffness. The deck is fiber glassed to the hull with a continuous, reinforced gusset that runs along the entire length of the deck-to-hull seam inside the boat and is formed of multiple layers of cloth and epoxy to create a single piece monocoque shell. When other boats come apart while being battered against rocks or pilings following a grounding or other such calamity, the deck usually unzips from the hull leading to instant loss and disaster. Loss due to a deck-hull separation will not happen to a CCS boat.

The mast is securely stepped directly on the keel, not on the deck where support is far more tenuous. The chain plates that provide anchoring points for the shrouds that support the mast are embedded into the heavy gusset that encircles the boat just below the deck and will never rip out.

Now for the special mods. The deck and cockpit were given a dark green color that is easier on the eyes in bright, glaring sunlight than lighter pastel colors, and is more visible in the fog than the lighter colors. Toe rails were increased in cross section for improved footing. The slender toe rails of the Bull's Eye lead me to make this change in my Goldeneye. A small glass port was installed on either side of the cabin top for side visibility from within the cabin. The mast was tapered for purely aesthetic reasons.

Anchoring and mooring required special consideration. A single deck cleat was replaced by two Herreshoff design cleats. The Herreshoff cleats are less apt to snag feet than conventional cleats and are easier under foot when stepped on as often happens with deck cleats. The Herreshoff cleats also offer more versatility in securing lines and are less prone to shedding improperly tied lines. When leaving an anchored boat unattended for any length of time, such as overnight or in heavy weather, two anchors of different types should be deployed. Never fasten two anchor lines to the same cleat. A separate cleat should be available for each line so that each line can be adjusted or removed, as needed, without interfering with the other. Mooring pennants are often provided in pairs for safety. They too should always be on separate cleats.

My primary anchor is a five-pound Hi-Tensile Danforth. The forged Hi-Tensile has thinner flukes than the standard sheet metal anchor and has beveled edges enabling the Hi-Tensile anchor to engage a hard bottom more effectively than the thicker, blunt-edged standard. I have used both extensively, and the difference is dramatic. However, in some circumstances, a bare hand can be the best device to engage a soft bottom. The Danforth is stowed on deck in teak chocks with quick-release pins for easy access. Both ends of the stock are secured in teak chocks to prevent the anchor from fouling lines. A six-foot length of stainless steel chain runs from the stowed anchor through a chain (not a rope) deck pipe into the chain/rope locker below deck. When the anchor is stowed, most of the heavy chain hangs from a hook on the underside of the deck pipe cover to hold the cover securely in place in heavy seas. Rope deck pipe covers are not similarly secured. The chain is heavier than the anchor, but the weight of that chain holds the anchor line down when deployed to ensure that the tug on the anchor remains fairly horizontal, especially when short scope is required. Scope is the ratio of anchor line length being used to the water depth. Without the weight of the chain, the vertical angle of a short scope could dislodge the anchor from the sea floor. The chain also protects the nylon anchor line from chafing on sea floor debris.

My second anchor is a stainless steel, four-pound Bruce (made by Lewmar). I chose stainless for that anchor so it can be well cleaned for stowage below deck. The Bruce is better for rocky and grassy bottoms, the weakest areas for the Danforth.

Port and starboard sail locker covers and the main hatch cover are completely sealed with soft rubber gaskets to keep seawater out of the boat in heavy weather. Those covers are dogged down in the closed position with cam-action closures.

Of course, there are occasions when keeping seawater out of the boat is, at best, a pipe dream. For those, usually drama-filled moments, I installed two bilge pumps. One is electrical, the other a Whale Gusher hand pump. The hand pump is operated from the cockpit where no hatches have to be opened to get at it. I added those pumps knowing full well that, in the real world, the principle means of offloading unwanted water is often a highly motivated matey armed with a bucket.

Cabin and hull ventilation was addressed to maximize creature comfort and to prevent mildew to the extent possible. A small, twelve-inch square, Lewmar Ocean Hatch was installed on the forward deck for light and ventilation. This hatch can be opened wide or locked in a cracked-open position to allow air to enter without letting in rain or spray. A small stainless passive vent was added to the cabin top to ventilate that area. Another small Nicro solar-powered stainless ventilator was added to the aft deck to draw air through the entire boat. The solar-powered ventilator draws air into the boat through the chain deck pipe, forward hatch (if cracked open), cabin top vent, and main hatchway door louvers to purge the boat of accumulating heat and moisture from internal evaporation.

Fresh water will always evaporate leaving the boat perfectly dry. Salt is a moisture magnet. Anything that has been wet with salt water and not rinsed off with fresh water will dry in the sun but will become soaked again as soon as the humidity returns. For this reason, every effort is made to keep seawater out of the cabin. We do not even enter the cabin if we are wet with salt water. Anything we may need while underway is kept either in the cockpit or within arms' reach inside the cabin. Only the forward chain/rope locker, where used anchor line is stored, is allowed to stay wet with seawater.

Inside the cabin two soft reading lights are positioned, one over each bunk, where they will not interfere with night sailing. Two teak bookcases are attached to the hull over the port bunk for reference material such as equipment manuals and navigational aids. Cape Cod Shipbuilding provides an equipment shelf over each bunk. I added a nylon net hammock to each shelf as a "keeper" so that stored items are not bounced out of the shelves in rough seas. Those hammocks are a must!

An equipment shelf was added to the port sail locker along with a teak peg rack for organizing lines. The equipment shelf contains, in an organized fashion, the smallest critical items that are most easily lost or misplaced but are needed immediately when they are needed and are often needed at night. The equipment shelf has dedicated holes for two flashlights and a rechargeable searchlight. A rechargeable wireless mike for the VHF radio resides on the shelf in its docking station along with my cell phone and the handle for the hand bilge pump. Two twelve-volt outlets for the rechargeables are located below the shelf. The peg-rack has six pegs that hold safety-harness tethers, reefing lines, dock lines, a dinghy painter, and spare lines. The remaining space is filled with life jackets and fenders. No sails are kept in the port sail locker. They fill the starboard locker.

Two Kidde 5-BC fire extinguishers are located, one in the cabin and one in the starboard sail locker where at least one is reachable from inside the cabin and from the cockpit.

An EPIRB (Emergency Position Indicating Radio Beacon) is fastened to the aft deck adjacent to the engine hatch. In the event that the boat is overwhelmed with water and begins to sink, at a depth of four feet below the surface, the EPIRB will be automatically released (ejected by a stiff spring) from its housing and float to the surface. This device will immediately begin transmitting emergency signals to three satellite systems. One is a high altitude geostationary system (GEOSAR) that receives the signal and instantly retransmits it back to earth alerting 24-7 monitoring stations (LUTs or Local User Terminals) of an emergency somewhere on the planet. That signal contains my name, boat identity, and description. The second is a low altitude, fast-moving system of satellites (LEOSAR) that will locate my position using Doppler technology. Those satellites circle the earth once every one hundred minutes, which is the amount of time that it could take to pinpoint my position. The third is the GPS satellite system, which provides real time and continuous tracking of my exact position in terms of latitude and longitude coordinates. Since my EPIRB has GPS capability, the GEOSAR system will instantly receive (in addition to my name, boat identity, and description) the exact location of my imminent demise, thus speeding up the rescue process. Each crew member on my boat has a PLB (Personal Locator Beacon) with GPS capability attached to an inflatable life vest. The PLB performs the exact same function as the EPIRB. The life vest is worn at all times while under way in case of a man overboard event, except near shore in the calmest weather. We probably should wear them all the time, but we don't on quiet days near shore since the boat has lifelines. I do wear a life vest all the time when single handing.

Now for the sails. How much modification can be done to the sails? Well, quite a bit, actually, and I'm only cruising with the boat, not racing it. Let's start with the main. CCS equips the Goldeneye mainsail with luff and foot ropes that feed into slots in the mast and boom respectively. This arrangement leaves no gaps between the sail and the spars, which is efficient aerodynamically, but unfortunately, not very efficient from almost any other point of view. The Bull's Eye was also equipped this way. Whenever I wanted to reef the Bull's Eye's mainsail, I had to lower the sail about three feet to wrap it around the boom in roller-reefing fashion. The lowered sail would force the bottom three feet of luff rope to slip out of its groove in the mast allowing the entire bottom three feet of sail to drape below the boom creating a visibility and mobility hazard during most of the reefing process. Should the halyard be dropped, even for an instant, the entire mainsail would drop into the cockpit and have to be rethreaded into the mast groove. None of this is pleasant in conditions requiring a reefed sail. Furthermore, while underway, with no openings between the boom and the sail, one cannot grasp the boom securely for support to perform such necessary personal functions as, say, relieving oneself over the side. These things do have to be considered, you know. Also, a mainsail with luff and foot ropes cannot be properly furled onto the boom when not in use and, therefore, must be removed, bagged, and stored.

Sail slides were attached to the luff and foot ropes of my Goldeneye's mainsail. The slides engage the same grooves intended for the ropes. Being able to grasp the boom securely by wrapping one's hand over the top of it and under the sail (between sail slides) is a real convenience whenever handling that part of the rig. The openings between the sail and the boom also allow sail stops (ties) to be placed where needed prior to lowering the mainsail completely for furling.

Jiffy reef grommets were added to the sail along with a hook on the boom for the forward grommets. Turning blocks and cleats were added to the boom for reefing lines to draw down the aft grommets. One fore-and-aft pair of grommets was positioned about two feet above the boom for a first reef and a second pair about four feet up for a second reef. I think the second reef is available only to make the crew feel somewhat secure in weather so extreme that most everyone aboard is convinced they are all going to die. I have come to this conclusion after experiencing totally terrifying conditions in which the first reef was entirely adequate. A jack line was added to the lower portion of the sail to allow the sail to pull away from the mast for reefing. The jack line is a single line that laces the lower one-third of the sail to the mast slides. When the sail is raised, the jack-line pulls tight and holds the sail close to the mast. When the sail is partially lowered for reefing, the jack line goes slack, permitting the sail to fold down onto the boom. Nothing has to be disconnected from the mast. Without the jack line, the lower slides would have to be slid out of the mast groove creating the same potential problems that I had with the Bull's Eye's luff rope, including the risk of dropping the entire sail into the cockpit.

A No. 6 Lewmar winch was added to the cabin top for the main halyard, making proper tensioning of the halyard easier than with no winch, especially for a vintage seaman. The matching jib halyard winch is standard issue.

Three special purpose jibs were purchased, in addition to the working jib, for the Goldeneye: a storm, a very large (160 percent) Genoa, and a spinnaker. The storm jib's foot is raised over a foot above the deck so that it will not scoop up water in rough seas. That raised foot proved to be a real blessing. Even the working jib tends to scoop water in steep waves and throw it aft into the cockpit. This tendency may be more of an issue for small boats than for larger ones. Four self-tailing, No. 14 Lewmar winches service the jib sheets; two of the winches are dedicated to the spinnaker.

I chose not to install a roller reefing / furling (r/f) jib for the following reason. Knowing the long hours that would be spent beating to windward, I wanted no compromise in sail efficiency. Even fully extended, the roller r/f jibs do not fit properly, especially as they age. Those areas continually exposed to the sun and weather weaken over time, lose their shape, and distort the entire sail. Sailing with separate, dedicated purpose sails is like driving a stick shift car. I do that too.

One of the strongest disadvantages of using separate jibs is having to go forward in a seaway to take one down or put a new one on. To mitigate that handicap, I installed downhauls on all three windward jibs. Now I can douse any of the three jibs from the cockpit and sail with just the main if it is too rough to go forward and bend on a different jib.

Lifelines were installed on the Goldeneye but forward and aft pulpits were not. The forward pulpit would severely interfere with foredeck activities on this tiny boat, particularly those requiring access to the end of the bowsprit, such as for sail changes. A forward pulpit would also be a liability when anchoring. The lifelines were carried well fore and aft to provide adequate containment security during sail changes, which are done on one's knees for the most part. The kneeling position is also handy for multitasking, such as praying while tending sails on a bucking foredeck. Additionally, the absence of a bow pulpit permits lowering a sail directly onto the deck where it can be largely sheltered from the seas and where it does not obstruct the forward view. The bowsprit, extending forward beyond the pulpit, would create this issue. With a bow pulpit in place, the lowered jib would have to rise from the end of the bowsprit, over the pulpit rail, and back down to the deck. Without a bow pulpit, the jib can lay flat along the bowsprit and deck. There is no particular need for an aft pulpit. However, an aft pulpit could support a boarding ladder, a potential safety option. Unfortunately, such a little boat would look like a floating junkyard with all that claptrap hanging off the stern. The shrouds can support an unobtrusive boarding ladder if desired. The deck amidships is only about a foot off the water and is easily boarded from a swimming position. However, if fatigued or injured, a ladder could be necessary.

A canvass dodger was added to the cabin top for protection from wind and spray. The dodger has clear vinyl windows for visibility forward. The dodger also provides enough protection so that the main hatch cover can be left off for easy access to the cabin while under way. However, in heavy seas and strong winds, we found the need to keep the teak hatch cover in place as water can seep under the dodger when struck by boarding seas. In extreme conditions, green water can completely breach the dodger making the teak hatch cover essential.

The engine in this boat is a nifty affair. My eight-hp Yamaha, two-cycle outboard proved itself time and again to be the engine that can. I cannot say enough about this engine. It runs in any conditions, never quits, and always starts. The motor is not mounted on a bracket on the transom where the propeller would spend half its time out of the water in a chop and where the engine would inevitably snare the mainsheet while sailing.

This engine is located in a well under the aft deck, as low as possible, where the prop rarely, but occasionally, does come out of the water. The control arm was removed from the engine and replaced by a powerboat remote control located in the cockpit directly under the tiller. From this position I can easily shift from neutral to reverse or forward and accelerate in either gear. The engine cannot be rotated to steer, which is okay; the tiller can do that job adequately. The motor is equipped with electric start, an alternator to charge the battery, and a sailboat prop that increases reverse thrust by ducting exhaust bubbles forward when in reverse gear. By redirecting exhaust bubbles forward in reverse gear, the propeller blades can cleave onto "solid" water rather than a mixture of water and exhaust bubbles, thereby maximizing thrust. A special stainless fitting was fabricated to duct the idle exhaust overboard to avoid fouling the inside of the motor well. An eleven-gallon fuel tank is located in the bilge with a deck fill-pipe amidships on the starboard side and a remote fuel gage on the cockpit aft bulkhead. A nonsparking blower draws air from around the tank and exhausts it safely overboard.

This is the first boat I ever owned with an engine, so as a complete novice with the machine, I had to practice maneuvers that most boaters perfect as children. One of my first dockings under power resulted in a busted bowsprit fitting that left the bobstay hanging forlornly in the water like a limp penis. I'll spare you the grim details of that landing. Suffice it to say that this brilliant performance, a showstopper, occurred only one month before leaving on the subject adventure. Thanks to the cooperative support of Cape Cod Shipbuilding and Noank Shipyard, the destroyed fitting was replaced in a few weeks, and we left as scheduled. The irony of this event is that, during our trip, I lost the dinghy in rough seas off Chatham, Massachusetts, and had to dock the boat from that point on. I am now a substandard authority on docking a small sailboat under power—and that is being generous. Hard as it may be to believe, I am still more comfortable docking under sail than under power. Hopefully that will change because docking under sail is way too much work.

Built-in electronics include:

- A Garmin GPS mounted on a swing arm that holds the unit in the center of the companionway for perfect visibility from the tiller. The GPS can be swung out of the way in a flash to access the interior of the boat. The arm is stiff enough to hold the GPS steady in rough seas.

- Two Ritchie bulkhead-mount compasses are installed, one on either side of the companionway, thereby allowing the use of an alternate compass when the view of one compass is being obstructed by crew members sitting on the same side as the tillerman. Also, a compass is available directly in front of the tillerman from either the high or low side steering position. The original Danforth compasses were replaced because the red lights used to illuminate the white numerals on red compass cards at night resulted in pink numbers on a red background in effect rendering the cards unreadable and the compasses unusable for night sailing. The Ritchie compasses have green lighting on black cards with white numerals and are easily readable during twilight as well as after dark.

- A knot meter and a depth meter by Raymarine mounted, port and starboard respectively, on the cabin bulkhead just outboard of the compasses.

- A West Marine (Uniden) VHF radio mounted at the forward end of the cabin to minimize compass deviation. Unfortunately, that location is inaccessible from the cockpit. To establish practical access to the radio, a rechargeable, wireless handheld access microphone (WHAM) is mounted in its charger/docking station on the equipment shelf in the port sail locker. The WHAM can be carried in my pocket or on my belt for immediate use from anywhere on the boat. This little gem has a clear speaker, easy-to-read screen, and can perform almost any function available on the VHF directly, including programming. (It cannot turn the VHF on or off.) The VHF is connected to a whip antenna attached to the top of the mast.

· An Echomax radar reflector that constantly bounced against the mainsail when on a broad reach. I have no idea how effective it was, but we didn't get run over even in the shipping lanes. By contrast, a radar transponder is a small, unobtrusive cylinder that attaches directly to the top of the mast adding very little windage. A Sea-Me radar transponder will be added to the boat but was not installed in time for *Riding the Wild Ocean.* A radar transponder differs from a radar reflector in that, the transponder boosts the received radar signal from another vessel before returning the signal back to its source via the single transceiver antenna. The boosted signal (reflection) makes a little boat like mine look more like a small cruise ship on the radar screen of the sending vessel. At least that should make *Yvaledon* somewhat more visible to another boat or ship assuming, of course, that the radar is on and someone is actually looking at the radar screen.

Finally, a few comments about the dinghy: I selected a nine-foot, lightweight, hard-shelled dinghy to minimize drag under tow. The downside is that such a craft is relatively unstable when occupants are unseated and moving about, embarking and disembarking. I also chose to row the dinghy rather than use a small engine, again, to keep weight down, minimize drag, and to simplify operation. The towing attachment point was located midway up the stem from the waterline to the rail. High attachment points can result in capsizing the dinghy in steep, high seas. A painter made from floating rope is essential to prevent fouling the prop of the towing vessel. I carried two painters, a twenty-five-foot line for normal use, and a forty-footer for heavy weather to give the dinghy room to romp without charging (surfing) up the middle and crashing into my stern.[4]

Preparing the Crew

Having sailed around Cape Cod in a small, open craft once before, I knew what was needed to survive such an adventure. My life could easily depend upon my mate, should the worst happen. He would have to be of strong character, sound in body and mind, and above all, a man of unflinching integrity whom I could trust with my life. Of course, it would be nice if he liked sailing and actually wanted to go on such a crazy odyssey.

I had the perfect candidate. All I had to do was to con—uh, convince him to take the plunge into the most exciting adventure of his life. Unfortunately, he had never done anything remotely resembling what I was about to suggest. In fact, he had never ever sailed before in his entire seventy-three-year life span. The chances of his accepting were about as good as the chances of the ant moving that old rubber tree plant. Even if he did accept, would his wife threaten him with divorce if he went? This was going to be a white-knuckle proposal if there ever was one. But there was only one way to find out and that was to ask.

Lou LaFlamme, a colleague of mine at the engineering firm, Belcan, where we had been working for several years as engineering outsourcing suppliers to aircraft engine maker Pratt & Whitney following our retirement from Pratt, had shown a keen interest in my boat building project from day one. We also worked out at the local gym together. He became fascinated by the technical detail of every facet of the boat's design, construction, and

---

[4]   Further detail and comments describing our personal clothing and loose equipment carried aboard *Yvaledon* during the 2008 circumnavigation of Cape Cod can be found in Appendix B.

equipment. Lou had accompanied me on occasion to the Cape Cod Shipbuilding Company to see the boat under construction. Inviting him to crew for me around the Cape seemed so logical by the time we had reached that point in the boat's evolution; he had to say yes. Who else would I ask? Well, I asked and he said yes almost before I finished asking, pending approval from his home admiral. She consented. I did not inquire as to the specifics of their conversations on the matter. That was one sleeping dog I decided to let lie.

I asked Lou to jot down a few of his recollections at the time and of his training during the summer of 2008 prior to embarking on our journey around the Cape. He kindly submitted the following thoughts:

> Without any sailing experience or having any knowledge of the particulars of sailing and a complete lack of familiarity with sailboats, why did I do this and how did I prepare to do it?
>
> My interest began when I started discussing with Paul the building of his Herreshoff Golden Eye beginning some time in 2006 at Cape Cod Shipbuilding. I was enthralled with the details though I understood so little of what he was describing. Still, I was learning. The terms he was using to explain the various features of the boat were foreign to me. It was just like hearing another language. Yet, it was challenging. For me, this was an opportunity to embark into a new arena and I relished the chance to learn something new, but never expecting that it would lead to what it did.
>
> As the boat approached completion, Paul invited me to go with him to Cape Cod Shipbuilding. The purpose of the trip was for him to discuss with the builder certain features that needed clarification. But having me along was his intent to expose me to the real thing. I was tickled that he would invite me and I was truly pleased with what I saw. It was breathtaking.

When the boat was completed Paul moored it in Noank, CT in the fall of 2007. That fall Paul, for whatever reason, asked if I would be interested in sailing with him the following year. I jumped at the chance. But, and there is always a "but," we both needed to obtain proper gear and attire. Paul's stuff was outdated since he hadn't sailed for many years. So we set off to get what we needed. I relied on him exclusively but learned a lot. The clothes we purchased were lightweight tropical wear from base layer to waterproof outer wear. The personal gear was mainly safety and functional equipment. The items we purchased are listed in Appendix B. The total cost was well over $2,000 for each of us—an investment that proved its worth for the trip that Paul had proposed.

Knowing that we would be sailing the summer of 2008, I knew that I had to prepare for the eventuality of actually sailing. As I said earlier, what did I know about sailing? Well, for me, a complete novice, my task was to learn as much as I could about the craft of sailing. This started the prior winter, primarily, learning what I could by reading about sailing and plumbing the internet for more information. Whenever I came across something that was incomprehensible to me, I discussed it with Paul. He could clarify whatever was baffling to me either verbally or pictorially. We also spent time together doing one thing or another relating to ancillary tasks such as line splicing, knot making, navigating, chart reading, affect of ocean tides and currents, AD infinitum. There was so much to absorb with so little time to do it in. Paul had years of sailing behind him. I had zip! How was I to manage? And why was Paul so willing to take me on as a crew member? I viewed myself as a liability, not an asset for what we were about to embark on. Yet I persevered in spite of a certain amount of anxiety, needless to say. I was hungry for this new experience, optimistic and full of enthusiasm.

Well, the summer of 2008 had finally arrived and I was now going to experience my first sail. WOW! To this day I don't know how I managed that first sail. It was exhilarating. I did realize, however, that reading and talking about sailing is one thing. Actual sailing is another. All that preparation the past winter just seemed to escape me the minute I boarded the boat. Why, I couldn't even do a decent cleat hitch on my first try in spite of practicing it over and over during the past winter. How embarrassing. The one thing I did find out quickly was that I was comfortable in the boat, and the details I needed to remember came in time. We sailed about two days a week every week. Rarely did I take the tiller but I did manage the sails, hauling up the mainsail and the jib, resetting the jib with the sheets as requested, familiarizing myself with the charts and the various buoys, doing a bit of navigating and watching Paul handle the boat so expertly.

That summer we did put the boat through a number of trials just to see what it could do. And, I learned much. For one thing, that I was fast becoming a worthy crew member, which was an important achievement for one so new to the art of sailing. The experience of circumnavigating the Cape was second to none for me, this in an eighteen foot full keel sloop. Not many day sailors that we spoke to on the trip, and upon returning, said that they had attempted this, nor would they. Nothing more need be said except to offer my thanks to Paul for the chance of a lifetime.

Lou's interest in learning new and complex skills, his enthusiasm, athletic prowess, and tolerance for risk are all astonishing attributes for a man of his age. Yet there he was, as ready and eager as any young buck. I could not have asked for a better potential shipmate. However, there were still questions I had to have answered about the man. Could he perform under pressure? Would he panic in life threatening or perceived life threatening situations?

The Race, a hellish constriction at the end of Fishers Island through which the entire Long Island Sound empties and fills twice a day, would be the perfect venue for my diabolical little test. There, in over two hundred feet of water, the tidal current rushes to and fro creating a nasty rip that can easily be seen from a mile away. Selecting a day with a fresh fifteen-to-twenty-knot wind, I headed the boat toward the Race for Lou's first taste of fear afloat.

As we approached the Race from the protected western shore of Fishers Island, the churning rip seas in the Race around Race Rock became increasingly visible. The wild, six-foot, white water rapids looked larger than life. The closer we came the wilder they looked. Finally, Lou asked, "Where are we going?"

I said, "I thought we would sail around Race Rock. We need to know how well we can function under more demanding conditions. Here we can sail into and out of those conditions as we wish."

Silence!

We sailed past Race Rock on a starboard tack, well out of reach of the strong current to avoid being washed into the Rock itself. We then jibed to approach the Race on a port broad reach. The wind was from the SW at fifteen to twenty knots, and the current was ebbing to the SE at over three knots. I began to feel the boat getting sucked into the racing water, the white noise of the rip rising to a frightening crescendo. Whirlpools of spinning surface water dotted the sea, flattening the water between steep, tumbling waves. Suddenly a huge wave slammed into the starboard side drenching everything and us and twisting the boat to port. The bow rose to the sea all but stopping forward progress. I ordered Lou to crank in the luffing working jib so that I could fall off slightly to get the boat going again. He obeyed instantly. After stabilizing the boat, I informed Lou that we were going to sail a 360-degree circle to test the boat on all points of sail in those conditions and was he all right with that?

"Yes" came the reply.

The first maneuver was to turn the boat counterclockwise into the wind and tack. Lou had to prepare the sheets while taking heavy spray and hanging on for dear life. The tack was generally into the current, yet seas were toppling onto us from our aft quarters as well as from ahead. I warned Lou that if the tack failed, we would be thrown back onto our original tack and laid over on our beam ends. He was ready. The tack went as planned and we set up for the next task, a downwind jibe.

With a full main (unreefed), we were somewhat overcanvassed for those conditions, thus imposing a particularly challenging aspect to the intended jibe. Due to the wildly yawing boat, I was limited as to how far I could pull in the main without accidentally jibing. With the wind on the starboard quarter, I pulled in the sheet as far as I dared without taking a knockdown, which wasn't very far. Then, timing the surging yaws, I pulled the sheet in as fast and as far as I could and let the next surge fling the boom over onto the starboard side for a port tack. The jib sheet ran free. As much as I could let the mainsheet run free, the wind still took the boat over onto its beam ends until I could swing it around onto a beam reach. The cockpit was awash with seawater sloshing around as violently as the sea around us. That event may have been more challenging for me than for Lou. However, we were done and headed back through the Race on a close reach against the current for calmer waters.

All told, we were in the Race for only thirty to thirty-five minutes, but I had my answers and I had a mate for the circumnavigation of Cape Cod on whom I knew I could rely.

CHAPTER X

AN UNSETTLING VEIL OF CALM

"Hey, Paul!"

Looking back over my shoulder, my ravishing hostess, Carol, stood in the doorway of her lavish summer home with a bottle of red wine in one hand, white in the other, her blonde strands of hair catching a hint of breeze.

"Red, thank you."

Turning back toward the view from the sun deck across a vast expanse of lush scrub pine, I could see the sea—shimmering, deep, blue, and serene; she lied and called to me like the insidious sirens of ancient literature. Her accomplice sun bathed me in early September warmth that could have relaxed the taught G-string of a violin, reducing it to the limp vestige of its primal cat gut. Most intoxicating was the stillness of the deck. Having arrived at this Nantucket oasis from Noank, Connecticut, after four days of constant bracing against the incessant motion of our sailing cockle shell, the stability of this land based shelf upon which I now stood seemed, somehow, not to be totally trusted—but it never moved!

At least one story below, my reverie was broken by the snapping of twigs as my sailing companion and dear friend, Lou LaFlamme, moved about taking pictures of Carol's house. Inside, a growing din of happy sounds accompanied the arrival of other guests, family and friends joining the party for days of swimming, sunbathing, and good-natured hell-raising. Why was I not caught up in the ambiance and festive mood of the occasion? Instead, my charts were laid out on the coffee table in the living room, my Eldridge Tide and Pilot Book open to the next day's tide and current tables. I knew that two days hence, Lou and I would be making our race for "the summit." The next two days would be spent here in total luxury regaining our strength at this, our "base camp," in preparation for our assault on "the summit": Butler Hole, Pollock Rip, and finally, the often savage, breaking inlet from the open sea across Chatham Bar into Chatham, Massachusetts—if we could find it. The sands off the Chatham coast shift so constantly that the NOAA charts provide no detailed data on depth or contour, just a warning note that also advises entry only with local knowledge. In an attempt to pick up some of that local knowledge, I had called the Coast Guard station at Chatham a few weeks earlier. The young man who answered the phone informed me that there indeed was a cut through the sandbar, marked by small orange flags, and used by the local fishing fleet. Perfect, how could I miss?

"How do you like Carol's house?" My dearest friend and wife, also named Carol, presented me with my glass of red wine. The two Carols, best of friends, had come over on the ferry from Hyannis a few days earlier to prepare for the festivities. I told her I loved it. We walked together into the house to greet the newly arrived guests and to begin a feast of hors d'oeuvres, a sumptuous sit-down dinner, and of course, more wine. The wine, along with other select beverages, greased the skids for increasingly animated and noisy conversation until well into the evening on this late summer day in 2008.

CHAPTER XI

OVER THIRTY YEARS HENCE— POLLOCK RIP AND CHATHAM BAR REVISITED

It was 8:30 a.m.! The day's half shot! Sunlight filling the room, we have to get out of here! Emerging from a deep sleep, I quickly calmed down realizing that I had the whole day to eat, say good-bye, collect up our things, and buy some ice for the sail to Chatham. We weren't leaving until almost sunset hoping to arrive at Pollock Rip soon after sunup the next day. We had plenty of time. I made mental note of a breeze coming through the open windows that was a little brisk for that time of day, a matter of fact that I would later recall as an ominous sign.

Sounds from the kitchen told of breakfast preparations, relieving my anxiety of having missed breakfast altogether. I emerged upon a scene of people preparing and eating cold cereal from bowls while standing at the sink or counter or at any available table or other horizontal surface. Orange juice, milk, and coffee flowed freely. I joined the casual group for a dose of my own cereal, juice, and hot coffee. As breakfast ended, guests headed for the beach dragging the usual assortment of chairs, toys, and towels. The two Carols stayed behind preparing hearty sandwiches for the beach and for Lou and me to take with us to Chatham.

The radio and TV were forecasting strong winds for the next few days. The wind outside the house picked up steadily throughout the day. I had agreed to take my host Carol's brother, Bob, and her son, Ross, out to see the boat before we left. Ross drove us to the town dock. We got into the dinghy, and I began the half-mile row out to the moored boat. With three of us in the dinghy, the row against the stiffening breeze was a little more than I had bargained for, but there we were and not about to quit at that point. *Yvaledon* was already bouncing around in the choppy water as we arrived, so our visit was short. The row back was considerably easier than the row out with the breeze at our stern.

Back at the house, I checked the forecast again. Northeasterly winds turning to the north today were expected to pick up to twenty to thirty knots tonight with possible higher gusts and hold steady from the north for up to the next forty-eight hours. We would be sailing to the north directly into that wind for most of the night, tacking back and forth beating to windward constantly. This would be a wet and arduous sail. Would we survive Butler Hole and Pollock Rip in near gale force winds? Maybe we should wait a day or so to let things calm down. No! This is what we came out here for. This is the stuff real adventures are made of. The boat was capable, properly equipped, and we were trained. Now was not the time to shrink into a shell of fear and retreat from the very essence of the high adventure we had sought for so long. My mouth was dry. My decision was made, pending only Lou's concurrence.

Briefly describing to Lou what we were in for, I knew that he could not possibly understand ahead of time. I had exposed Lou to his first taste of harsh conditions in the Race at the entrance to Long Island Sound earlier in the summer. There, for about thirty minutes in twenty-knot winds and five-foot-high rip seas, on a sunny afternoon, I observed his reaction to the smashing waves and flying water tossing the boat about in every direction. No sign of panic was evident as he remained focused on his task of handling the jib sheets as we came about several times before sailing out of the rip current into calmer water. Now, with only that single, brief experience from which to extrapolate, Lou was willing to venture forth into the night if I were. His trust was remarkable. I could not fail him. Was I making the right decision or recklessly endangering his life (and my own)? I would know as we entered Pollock Rip. If the seas became unmanageable, I could retreat to the relative safety of Nantucket Sound. We would proceed at least that far.

Host Carol drove us —my wife Carol, Lou, and me—to the town dock where we picked up ice for the cooler and said our brief good-byes amidst the lengthening shadows of early evening. Loading ourselves and our gear into the dinghy, we began the long row out to *Yvaledon.* The wind had increased sufficiently to hold me to a pace that kept me pulling on the oars for thirty-five minutes to cover the half mile to *Yvaledon.* Winded with arms as limp as noodles, I grabbed *Yvaledon*'s rail and just rested for a few moments before transferring our parcels aboard the "mother ship." Having taken the precaution of donning our foul weather gear while still on the town dock, we were dry despite the soaking spray encountered on the way over.

Our preparations to leave quickly attracted the attention of the mooring patrol, ever alert to being ripped off by boaters eager to leave without paying their bills. A sturdy launch with three young men aboard pulled alongside and tied up to our boat. I asked and was granted permission to come aboard the launch. There I was informed that the two days for which I had already paid were to be supplemented with a third day's fee of $60 because I was eight hours into my third day on the mooring. I produced my MasterCard, which was promptly and efficiently processed by the onboard, digital, satellite-linked processing gadget. Responding to a question of where I was going at that time of day in such a little boat, my response elicited a form of, "Are you crazy?" reaction from the launch crew. Hoping that Lou had not noticed that repartee, I tried to assure them that we were not novices, and that I had done this before. Happy with their haul, the mooring police departed, leaving us to our fate.

We rigged the main with a single reef. I bent on the storm jib and tied it to the deck for later use. The reefed main alone would easily carry us out of the harbor where we could release the storm jib free of boat traffic. Traffic in and out of Nantucket Harbor is reminiscent of New York Harbor. Commercial ships, ferries, and yachts of all sizes vie for limited space in the narrow channel. On our way into Nantucket from Edgartown, Martha's Vineyard, several days earlier, we found ourselves sailing right through the middle of a sailboat race as the tightly packed fleet crossed the main navigation channel. I had to carefully avoid not only hitting any of those small craft but was further expected to position my boat within the fleet such that my sail wake did not foul the air of any of the racers. The latter expectation was conveyed by the anxious cries and flailing body language of the racing crews. The fact that I had the legal right of way in that channel was clearly irrelevant. With that recent experience still fresh in my mind, the engine and self-tacking mainsail without the jib seemed the best way to exit the harbor.

That was a mistake! Upon entering the exposed outer channel to the open sound, we found ourselves in a five-foot chop with a fifteen-to-twenty-knot wind streaking the water with foamy bubbles. Thirty miles of unbroken fetch from the Cape mainland was dumping the heavy seas into outer Nantucket Harbor. There was no way I was going to go up onto the deck to unleash the storm jib in that chop and risk getting soaked under my foul weather suit at the start of a long trek into the night. So there I sat, tiller in hand, making best possible headway against the wind and seas.

Sailing north toward the mainland, the shortening fetch gradually reduced the seas, making for more comfortable progress. The sun began to set as we passed Great Point on the northern tip of Nantucket. Preparations for darkness began with lunch. The sandwiches provided by the two Carols were a welcome respite. We stuffed ourselves knowing that may be our last chance at food before entering Chatham the following day. The teak companionway hatch cover was set in place in case the canvass dodger was breached or even swept away in heavy seas and possible gale force winds. Watching the remaining traffic out of Nantucket vanish to the west as we continued north underscored our sense of being alone in this vast watery wilderness. As darkness fell, we began trying to spot and identify navigation lights on shore and afloat. The GPS, set firmly on a swing-arm in the open companionway into the cabin, glowed warmly with our orange-colored course northward contrasting against a blue background. All was well.

Our first nighttime target was a flashing green four-second light on a floating buoy several miles north and west of Great Point. Since the wind was coming directly from that buoy, we had to tack either east or west of the mark. I chose a northwestward tack into deeper water. This buoy, marked "15," is positioned at the "fork-in-the-road" entrance to both Great Round Shoal Channel that runs off to the east, and the funnel-shaped lead-in to Butler Hole and Pollock Rip to the northeast. I sailed well past the point at which I could have tacked northeastward to make buoy "15" so that when I did tack, we could reach Butler Hole without any further tacking. I was also hoping that my extended northwestward track would permit us to sail a more relaxed close reach eastward rather than continue our slog hard on the wind. My intent was to skirt the southeastern edge of Handkerchief Shoal, which lay to the northwest of our course. I had to be extremely careful not to sail too far in a northwesterly direction before tacking eastward and running aground on the shoal. A northeastward track too far north of our desired course would take us into the shallow reef areas of Handkerchief Shoal little more than two or three feet deep several miles offshore. And

· Handkerchief Shoal is marked only by unlighted buoys, virtually useless at night.

SEPTEMBER 2, 2008, 10:42 P.M., TUESDAY:

"Ready about!"

"Hard alee!" I shouted as I pushed the tiller to leeward to redirect *Yvaledon* onto a northeastward (port) tack toward Butler Hole.

Seas had calmed down considerably with the shortened fetch although the wind had freshened noticeably. I eased the mainsheet slightly to accommodate our new heading, and spray across the cockpit shifted outboard ever so slightly but enough to ease our burden of constant dousing. Lou, at the forward end of the cockpit, was most relieved.

Hours passed. The southern tip of Handkerchief Shoal began to appear on the top of the GPS screen. We passed buoy "15" about two miles to the north of it on our starboard side. We began monitoring the depth meter more closely. The current was against us. Progress over the ground was painfully slow even with the strong wind. I noticed a slight swell building under the wind waves. Open ocean seas were being felt as they charged through Pollock Rip and Butler Hole, eventually dissipating in Nantucket Sound. We were heading smack-dab into them. I could not yet see our next mark, a flashing red four-second bell buoy about a half mile south of the tip of Monomoy Island. Over the horizon, I could see a faint white beacon flashing every ten seconds on the very tip of Monomoy. Although I could not see the beacon directly because it was below the horizon, I could see the scatter light reflecting in the moist atmosphere above the beacon.

Seas continued to build. We could not see them in the inky blackness of the night, but we could feel the boat charging up and down over the crests and into the troughs. The wind continued to increase, occasionally whistling in the rigging. The deep water was funneling into a narrowing band of navigable depth as Stone Horse Shoal closed in on the right from starboard, and

Handkerchief Shoal continued along our port side. The rate at which seas were building was somewhat alarming, but *Yvaledon* was making easy way through them. The engine was still running. I was afraid to shut it off because of electrical system problems we had experienced crossing Block Island Sound during the night of Wednesday, August 27. I did not want to lose the GPS, although had that happened, we were prepared to convert to more basic navigational techniques.

A new challenge was presenting itself. I was getting seasick. No sooner had I mentioned the problem to Lou, than I lightened my burden over the cockpit starboard coaming. Weakened by my condition, I asked Lou if he could take over the tiller so that I could recline onto the starboard seat. As was his nature, he jumped to the task without a moment's hesitation. Lou had taken the tiller several times earlier that evening and was ready again. There on the seat, with my head sheltered under the dodger, I found some relief. Minutes later, I was summoned back to the starboard coaming. Lying on my back again, weak with nausea, I knew that I would gradually recover as I always had in the past. For what seemed like hours, I lay there trying to regain enough strength to function. Lou had noticed that when I got seasick we were "meandering," so once I lay down and he took over the tiller, Lou, as he later noted, "glued onto the GPS and managed to get us back on track. My real concern was the narrowing of the channel in a building sea. That was a bit too risky for me."

The seas continued to build, the wind now shrieking. Lou began to express concern with the narrowing channel. On the GPS screen, he could see the shoals squeezing us on both sides. Our flashing red four-second buoy was clearly visible off the port bow as we rode over wave crests but disappeared in the troughs. Once again hard on the wind, we were going to slip safely past the red flasher mid-channel. The next buoy, a flashing green about a mile to the east, was directly in our path. We had to stay to the north of that buoy to stay within the channel. Missing that to the south would take us over shallow areas of sixteen to twenty feet at the northern end of Stone Horse Shoal, the channel being generally over forty feet deep between shoals. The concern over those shallows was not bottoming out against the sandy sea floor but encountering locally larger, steeper seas. I could tack to port to reposition into the channel but preferred to avoid that risky maneuver in those dark seas if possible. Lou could feel the seas still building. He began voicing his concern that he could not control the boat in the raging maelstrom. Suddenly he cried out, "You have to take the boat. I can't control it!" Having finally regained much of my strength, I took over the tiller as it became obvious that we would miss the green flasher by a few hundred feet south of the channel. The channel turned sharply eastward around the green flashing buoy permitting us to reenter the channel if we simply maintained our current heading. In short, we would cut across the northern end of Stone Horse Shoal on a brief excursion out of the channel and reenter the channel just past the green buoy.

The time was about 4:00 a.m. Dawn would soon be breaking. We braced for our shortcut across the northern tip of Stone Horse Shoal. A foul, two-knot current gradually slid us toward the right hand side of the channel, then out of it toward the Stone Horse shallows. I monitored the depth meter: thirty-eight feet… thirty-four…thirty…twenty-nine. The seas began responding to the rising bottom as they became noticeably larger and steeper… twenty-eight feet deep…twenty-six. White water spray began raining into the cockpit. Twenty-six…thirty…forty-one feet— we were back in the channel heading across Butler Hole!

Dawn began breaking. In the dim gray light of morn, I silently went into shock at the spectacle of the seas surrounding us. Although we had been in them for hours, we had not seen the seas before that moment. I had never been in anything like that in my life. Mountains of water nearly as high as my spreader, which is halfway up my thirty-foot mast, raced by. Every wave foamed with angry, writhing energy. Spray blew from every wave top into the next trough. There was no color in that predawn world, only bleak shades of gray.

"You went into shock, and I was awestruck!" recalled Lou. "I told myself, 'wonder of wonders!' and hung on. I knew this was going to be a ride of rides, but I was truly calm through it all. I never lost faith in the captain. What a thrill! My main task at this point was to keep the cockpit as dry as I could, which was an arduous task at that."

We had been ignoring the pressure building in our bladders, not wanting to address the issue in those seas. Normally, we could have relieved ourselves over the side from a standing position either on the seats or on the deck—but not in those seas. With forces strong enough to pitch us over the side, we were forced to perform that function from a kneeling stance on a seat, firmly braced against the cockpit coaming while securely grasping a lifeline stanchion in one hand and one's self in the other.

For the first time since the previous day, I could see the dinghy. At the end of its forty-foot tether, wave tops, parted by the dinghy's high-riding bow, jumped into the air in a fountain of spray briefly obliterating the dinghy from view. The little boat then dashed back into sight as it cascaded down the back side of a wave only to rise again on the next wave and repeat the performance. My comical little dinghy broke the tension as we watched its antics behind us. How it managed to stay afloat through all the action of the night, I will never know.

By 6:30 a.m., the current was going slack in Pollock Rip in preparation for flooding east. We were emerging from Butler Hole heading toward the deep waters of the open Atlantic. Monomoy Island and the Cape Cod mainland stretched northward. Chatham lay at the southeastern corner of the Cape directly north of Monomoy. Between us and calmer open water lay Pollock Rip Channel, two miles of twenty-to-thirty-foot deep water roiled with swirling currents and incoming ocean swells and whipped to a froth by the stiff north wind. On either side lay deadly, unseen reefs and the scattered remains of dozens of hapless boats and ships. As the slack current began to flood, carrying us with it, the moving water heading east from Nantucket Sound into Butler Hole and Pollock Rip turned north in and around Pollock Rip to run parallel to the coastline. There, in Pollock Rip, where the incoming ocean swells meet the turning, swirling tidal currents, strange things happen.

The incoming swells were entering Pollock Rip, generally from the east, at different speeds and from slightly different directions due to the drag of the uneven and shallow bottom contours. This resulted in colliding mountains of water. Where crests invaded troughs, relatively flat seas ensued. Where merging crests and troughs coincided, huge rogue waves formed with spectacular results. Superimposed on this were the twisting, churning current and the unrelenting north wind. For us, the current became a mixed blessing. While sweeping us forward in the general direction of our intended route, the current was running against the incoming ocean swells causing them to steepen and topple. Rip seas of this nature are normally formed by tidal currents and wind running in opposing directions, causing the wind driven seas to steepen and topple. In Pollock Rip, the wind from the north set up its own wave pattern of ten-to-twelve-foot seas, which ran at right angles to the heavier ocean swells entering from the east against the current from the west. Into this mad turmoil we plunged on a magnetic (compass) heading of sixty degrees.

At least it was daylight. We could see the enemy.

Again, Lou recounted his impressions: "All I perceived at this time was a sea with an incomparable rage not truly understanding the forces in motion to cause it, and I wasn't about to ask questions of the captain then."

The sudden change in depth from forty-plus feet of water in Butler Hole to less than thirty feet in Pollock Rip was immediately felt. Seas began striking the boat at odd angles sending water into the cockpit and over our heads into the sail. My first instinct was to try and find a way to contact each wave in a manner that would minimize the water taken into the cockpit. But that had to be done without too much sacrifice to our heading and ground track. The rogue waves were the worst. They seemed to travel in pairs and caused us to lose ground, but the rogues were usually followed by relatively flat seas where we could recover the lost ground. As I began to recognize wave forms that would slam into the bow and dump heavy amounts of water into the cockpit, I became somewhat adept at swinging the bow away just enough to soften the blow and allow most of the collapsing wave top to slide under the hull rather than crashing against it. I could not spot or react in time to them all, and for that, I was always punished. Actually, Lou was punished; he did the bailing!

So intent was I on dancing with the waves, I never saw it coming. Seemingly out of nowhere, a solid green sea, moving upwind, came over the low (starboard) rail at shoulder height and marched right into the cockpit, dumping the greatest amount of water we had taken aboard so far. Where the hell did that come from? Meanwhile, the steep swells kept coming at the bow. Now I had to keep an eye to starboard as well as forward. We could not take another one of those. As the huge ocean swells collided, they occasionally squeezed out secondary waves, like peas from a pod, sending them upwind until they spent themselves in a futile drive against all the forces working against them. We just happened to get caught in the path of one of those secondaries. I saw the next one and modified my dance accordingly, swinging the stern away from the sea allowing the invading wave to slide sweetly under the hull. On and on we danced. Two miles never seemed so far! But the roughest ride was still ahead.

The end was in sight: a huge red gong buoy marking the pinch point of Pollock Rip Channel and its exit to the clear, deep, open Atlantic. Around the buoy lay water between ten and thirty feet deep, the deepest path being through about twenty-six feet of water around the south side. Our course around the south side of the buoy would take us over one or more submerged wrecks not visible from the surface but identified on the chart. Fourteen-foot seas would reduce the water depth in the wave troughs from twenty-six to nineteen feet, each wave being half above and half below the nominal surface level. Water depth in Pollock Rip had been averaging roughly twenty-six to thirty feet. I glanced at the depth meter and compass whenever I could take my eyes, just for an instant, off the attacking waves.

Twenty-three feet deep…twenty-two…twenty-one… now every foot lost in depth made a huge increase in wave height and steepness. *Yvaledon* soldiered ahead. Lou bailed for his life! The bailing, he later mused, "was continuous and feverish. But I was truly calm throughout, just busy." Twenty feet…nineteen…Seas crashed against the bow lifting it to an alarming angle and then swept over the cabin and dodger into the reefed main dragging the boat over onto its side and spilling out of the sail back into the ocean. Dear God, when will this end?

The oncoming seas, having risen to at least fifteen feet in height, were traveling so fast and were so steep that as the boat lifted to rise to each occasion, the buoyancy accelerated the boat upward pressing me down into my seat with a force that made my 150-pound frame feel more like two hundred pounds. At the top of each wave, the wind would strike the sail with its full force, after having been somewhat sheltered in the previous trough. The boat would lay over and plunge into the next trough while shedding hundreds of pounds of water. Those rip seas were so much more terrifying than simple wind driven seas of the same height! The confused rip seas lacked the symmetry of ordinary wind waves. As a result, the boat would be slammed unexpectedly by the huge waves, violently jolting our bodies in random directions for which we were never fully prepared or properly braced. I struggled to control my panic, fighting an urge to jump over the side to get away from the violence and noise and terror aboard the boat. Somehow, the distant sea several hundred feet away seemed calmer, quieter—even safer—than the madness in our wretched boat. Such irrational impulses are surely the product of sheer panic. I think I now have a better understanding of how and why yachts, particularly racing yachts, have been found floating in calm seas, completely intact, after a storm with no one aboard.

I began to think of how we would release our harness tethers and clear ourselves of the boat safely as it went down and sank beneath the waves. Would the EPIRB release from its spring-loaded mount on the aft deck at the four-foot depth of submersion, float up to the surface, and automatically start transmitting our distress and position as it is designed to do? Did we still have our PLBs (Personal Locator Beacons) on us? Would they work in the violent seas or would the white water smother the signal? Could we contact the Chatham Coast Guard station while floating in the water? How long could we survive in the cold water? Would the raging seas overwhelm us so that we could not breathe in the white water? In my panic, my imagination was running away with me. I had to get a grip, stay focused! As bad as things were, we were not taking on serious water into the cockpit.

Twenty-three feet...Twenty-seven...forty! Yes! We were free at last. The seas calmed down rapidly as we left Pollock Rip behind. The huge rip seas of the shallow channel gave way to relatively gentle ten-to-twelve-foot, deep water wind waves. The two-knot current became a meandering, almost unnoticeable half knot or less. The twenty-five-to-thirty-knot wind seemed like a zephyr. Now all we had to do was find the entrance to Chatham Harbor. The sun was shining. It never felt so good to be alive!

My dear friend and sailing companion, Lou LaFlamme, never knew of my fear in Pollock Rip Channel until reading this account of that harrowing passage. His courage was unshakable.

"I should mention," he insists, "that my 'unshakable' courage was based on my faith in the captain. I never doubted for a minute that we would get through this."

Still on a magnetic heading of sixty degrees, we continued seaward for about seven miles until we could tack back toward Chatham to our northwest. As we proceeded, our first boat sighting since we left the Nantucket traffic lanes the day before came into view. At first, all we could see was a distant cloud of seagulls on the horizon. Then a small fishing boat began to appear beneath the seagulls. Eventually, we passed within a few hundred feet of one another. The thirty-five-foot boat disappeared into every trough. Even its vertical exhaust stack and roof antenna disappeared from view. The crew all waved to us as they passed. They were headed for Chatham. I so wanted to turn around and follow them in but knew that we could never keep up with them. That was the first and last vessel we saw that day before eventually entering Chatham Harbor.

At the end of our northwest tack back toward Chatham, we came within hearing distance of the large whistle buoy marking the general location of Chatham Harbor. About a mile offshore, that buoy was to become our base of operations in our search for the cut through Chatham Bar into the harbor. I knew that sooner or later a fishing vessel would either come out of or go into the harbor thereby identifying the exact position of the cut, but I was in no mood to sit out there in rough seas and wait. The young man at the Coast Guard station to whom I had spoken over the phone a few weeks earlier had informed me that the cut was marked by small orange flags on floating buoys on either side of the channel. Such tiny markers would be invisible in those seas until one was practically on top of them. The chart was of no use because the entire Chatham area is undocumented due to constantly shifting sands. The search was further frustrated by the comber field, a continuous band of breaking ocean swells one half to three quarters of a mile wide extending for fifty miles northward along the beach from Chatham to Provincetown. One does not sail into or through the comber field. Lou and I carefully began our search from the whistle buoy staying at least two to three hundred yards beyond the outer limits of the combers. Beating our way northward, we scanned the surf for a telltale break in the combers. This could be a long search, but the cut had to be reasonably close to the whistle buoy. However, I did not know whether the cut was north or south of the buoy.

As we focused our attention on the surf to our left, my eye caught sight of an unusual line of white water to our right. Our worst fear was about to be realized.

A large rogue wave had begun to break over a mile offshore, well outside of the established comber field, trapping us between it and the field. The wave was hundreds of feet long, making escape around it impossible. The question was not how to evade it but how to engage it. I dared not let that magnificent surfing wave hit us broadside or even at an angle lest the curl twist us completely broadside and broach the boat, rolling it over and jamming the top of the mast into the shallow sandy bottom assuring a dismasting. I also wanted to put as much distance between us and the comber field as possible prior to diving into that curling green giant. With the engine at full power—Yes, the engine was still running!—and the sail properly set for maximum speed, we headed east directly into the teeth of that thing. At closer range I could see that there was no danger of being pitch poled end-over-end backwards; the wave was too small for that. But the wave was all green water with only a small toping of decorative froth. At only about six feet in height, the rogue wave was traveling westward crossing at right angles to a sea of ten-to-twelve-foot wind waves that were moving southward. That curling monster, though smaller than the surrounding wind waves over which it was riding like a great snake, was still going to swallow us whole.

"My reaction to this monster rogue wave," as Lou recollected, "was awsh——! And I hung on hoping for the best. What else could anyone have done? But, here again, I never had any thought that we wouldn't get through this. Why should I have? It was just another eventful happening! However, there sure was a lot of bailing that was necessary after that one."

As contact became imminent, the world went into slow motion, as before a pending auto accident. I watched the bowsprit disappear into the vertical wall of water about halfway up the wave. Then the entire forward deck vanished, rising as if to reach for a gasp of air. Just before the water hit the dodger, I ducked for shelter behind the cabin. All went briefly dark as the wave unloaded its burden upon us.

As quickly as it came, the overriding rogue wave was gone. Left behind was a shuddering *Yvaledon* with her cockpit swimming in water, a stunned but unharmed crew, and incredibly, the dodger still intact supported by its stainless steel frame. But every snap holding the dodger to the cabin top had come undone. The engine was still running!

Hardly had we regained our senses, when a sudden jolt, as if we had hit a rock, stopped all of the boat's remaining forward motion and then some. Yet I knew we had hit nothing; there was nothing out there to hit. Lou grabbed the free end of a piece of line attached to the aft starboard cleat and presented it to me, half playfully and half dumbfounded, with the question, "What's this?" The pathetic, limp, frayed end of the line hung forlornly from his fist. He knew full well that he was holding the dinghy painter or what was left of it. When the rogue wave was done with us, it attacked the dinghy, immediately swamping and ripping it from its mother ship. The shock we felt was the 2,300-pound test line snapping as the dinghy was torn from *Yvaledon*'s grasp. With four eyes riveted aft, no sign of the dinghy was visible, only the retreating rogue wave. The dinghy had not sunk, because of full floatation built into its seats, so the wave must have kept rolling the little craft along all the way to the beach where it was either ground to dust or blown clear of the surf. I guess we will never know.

Now the game had changed. We no longer had our shore tender. Anchoring or picking up moorings were no longer options. We had to dock wherever we pulled in to resupply. However, we had a more immediate concern. We still needed to find the cut through Chatham Bar. With plenty of daylight left, we had ample search

"Hang on, Lou!"

time remaining.The day was too young to expect the return of fishing boats, and we had taken one beating after another since leaving Nantucket. In short, I was building a case to cheat. I reached for my WHAM mike to call the coast guard and ask for a heading from the whistle buoy to the cut. The WHAM is a Wireless Handheld Accessory Microphone that connects the user to the ship's VHF radio from anywhere on the boat. Since the VHF is safely tucked away inside the cabin, I had no inclination to open a hatch in that seaway to get at it. The WHAM mike was a perfect solution. Mutiny from the crew opposed to a cheating captain was not to become a problem on that day. Lou all but flung open the port sail locker and handed me the mike.

"*Yvaledon* to Chatham Coast Guard, *Yvaledon* to Chatham Coast Guard, come in please."

"*Yvaledon*, this is Chatham Coast Guard."

"I am in an eighteen-foot sailboat near the whistle buoy looking for the channel across the bar into the harbor, marked by little orange flags. Can you give me a heading from the buoy to the cut, over?"

"I'll be out there in fifteen minutes. Meet me at the whistle buoy. You can follow me in."

"Thank you very much!" Then my radio went dead, but the message had been sent.

Within five minutes, I saw the brightly colored coast guard launch leaving the harbor headed toward the inner end of the cut. As he turned into the cut, my first question was answered. The cut was north of the whistle buoy. At that point, he could have returned to his dock, and I would have been able to head safely into the harbor. However, an assist was in motion and would be completed. I began heading north to meet him. Within a few hundred feet and closing, I could see him trying to contact me with his VHF. I waved to him with my mike trying to convey that my radio was dead. He understood and came closer to within hailing distance. I confirmed that my radio was dead. He told me to follow him. I told him I would have to tack against the wind. Again, he understood, and off we went. I noted our heading from the whistle buoy to the cut entrance.

"My thought at this point," remembers Lou, "was that the coast guard was being overly concerned for our safety. But then, to their credit, they had no notion who they were dealing with nor what our sailing craft was like and were taking no chances. We were in a heavy sea in a vessel that could have been perceived as not worthy of this sea and in an area fraught with hazards."[5]

Making a sharp left turn, *Yvaledon* accelerated onto a broad reach into the cut. A large coast guard helicopter circled overhead keeping us at the center of its circles but carefully keeping enough distance to prevent its downwash from interfering with our sails. We did not see the little orange flags amidst the white foamy surface until we were within about one hundred feet of the first one. Although the seas were not breaking in the inlet, they were surging heavily. The thirty-five-foot launch was having difficulty moving slowly enough to keep us near. Each sea that surged into her twisted her sideways as the next sea surfed us headlong at her broadside. We could hear the launch engine rev up and watch the launch bolt ahead as the captain straightened her out to maintain his heading and to prevent us from coming aboard boat and all. Thus, we proceeded into the harbor.

Once inside Chatham Bar, the calm seas were a welcome relief from the open water we had just left behind. The wind was still whipping at us. Lou lowered the main and tied it to the boom. Now under power alone, we began our search for a dock. The

---

[5]   Once again, I have included an aerial photograph, shown in Appendix F, of the current configuration of Chatham Bar to assist the reader with visualizing our track. Notice how different the bar area looked in 2008 compared to 1977, as shown in Appendix D—courtesy of the severe storms during that thirty-three-year period

launch and the helicopter had disappeared. After a mile or so, we saw a gathering of boats near the shore, which looked like a commercial area. We headed in that direction through a private mooring field toward a small floating dock. Pulling up to the dock, we tied up to one side and sat there in the cockpit like stunned fish waiting for something we knew not what. Gradually we began to move, as we strained to summon any grain of energy left in our pathetic, exhausted bodies to begin the seemingly impossible effort of cleaning up the mess aboard the boat, drying things out, and finding some place to shower, sleep, and eat— possibly in that order.

CHAPTER XII

CHATHAM AND THE RACE TO PROVINCETOWN WITH TROPICAL STORM HANNAH

The first visitors to our berth at the floating dock, which turned out to be part of the Chatham town pier, were a pair of large seals that surfaced only a few feet from the boat, playfully rolling over and generally looking for attention, which of course they got. They remained with us for the duration of our stay in Chatham. I think they had actually become voting residents, as well as official greeters, of the town.

Looking around, we soon realized that we had also arrived at the Chatham Fish Pier. The coast guard launch that had retrieved our sorry hides lay at her berth adjacent to the fish pier along with two other coast guard vessels. Tied up to the innermost, or shoreward, side of the square floating dock was a small, open motor launch identified as "harbormaster." That boat shared space with a long foot ramp that ascended to the parking lot. *Yvaledon* took up the entire south side of the small dock. The two other sides were empty. The pier itself was busy with fishing vessels gassing up, loading water and ice, or unloading fish and hosing off. The small floating dock where we were berthed was used by the fishing boats to tie up while waiting for a spot at the main pier. There boats could also hose down with fresh water or fill onboard tanks. We were clearly taking space normally reserved for the fishing fleet, not to mention using the only fresh water hose on the floating dock. However, with no dinghy, I could see no other option.

Having seen the commotion caused by our coast guard escort into the harbor, several townspeople began drifting down to the dock area to see what was going on. By that time, we had begun spreading things out on the dock to hose them off with fresh water and to let them dry out in the sun, so it became quite evident that we probably had something to do with the commotion. The questions soon started. Each answer we gave increased the inquisitiveness of our visitors until Lou and I had to stop working and devote full time to satisfying the insatiable curiosity of the small crowd that had gathered on the little dock. As a few people exited up the ramp to the parking lot, new visitors descended to take their place. Eventually, more people left than arrived, and Lou and I could resume our work on the boat. One man, who had left and come back several times, noted that this was the first sailboat to enter the harbor in years. That certainly explained, at least in part, the unusual level of interest in our boat and our journey.

One of the visitors asked us how long we planned to stay at the dock. That question startled me a little, tensing my nerves. He was not one of the casual onlookers, yet I did not know who he was. I presumed he was an official of some kind and worded my answer very carefully. I told him that we were on a long journey and had lost our dinghy in the combers on the way into the harbor. As a result, we were forced to dock, as opposed to anchoring or taking a mooring but that we would leave as soon as we had rested and restocked our stores. He then identified himself as the harbormaster and asked again when we would be able to leave. He further explained that the limited dock space was used by the fishermen when the pier was busy. I asked if we could stay for two nights and leave as soon as possible the second day, adding that if a fisherman asked me to leave to make room for him at the dock, I would do so. I went on to implore that I had hoped to sleep ashore rather than in the small wet boat. He grinned and agreed to my proposal. Later that evening, we were visited by the second shift, or night harbormaster, who asked the same question. I explained that the day master had given us permission to stay for two nights. He seemed surprised but also agreed to the arrangement. Our agreement with the day harbormaster had apparently not risen to the level of importance necessary to make the agenda for day-night shift coordination. But the sun was setting and all was well.

Our things had dried fairly quickly on the sunny dock, but the boat was still a salty mess inside. That would have to wait for the morrow and another day of sunshine. Our drying gear was returned to the boat and locked up for the night. Off we went into town—on foot—not exactly the manner in which two celebrities such as we should be traveling, but one must sometimes deal with untoward indignities as the harsh realities of life impose. A mile and a half of mostly uphill and downhill lead into town and to the Cranberry Inn, a place I had been before, almost a lifetime ago. On the way, a small pickup truck stopped to inquire as to our destination. We immediately recognized the repeat visitor to our boat earlier that afternoon. Following our spontaneous whoop of recognition, he offered us a ride. We threw our boat bags into the bed of his truck and jumped in squeezing into the tiny cab next to him. Off we went. After being dropped off at the inn, we thanked him for the ride and waved him off. We walked along a short walkway with well-manicured grass on both sides, up a few steps, across the porch and into the lobby where we registered at the desk. We were directed to our room where we showered, got into some dry clothes, and made our way to the lounge. Let me tell you, there is nothing in this world to make a man feel more civilized after a long trek of any kind than a hot shower and clean, dry clothes! Having seated ourselves across from the great stone fireplace in the pine-paneled study lined with shelves of books, a middle-aged woman (young to us) appeared and offered us a choice of adult beverages while we waited to be seated in the dining room. I had arrived in heaven—again.

The next morning, after nine or ten hours of sleep, maybe even a little more, we walked into the dining room to be seated in the most delightful area with sun pouring through the many windows and an open door welcoming in the smell of fresh flowers and honeysuckle. Fresh fruits, cereal, a variety of juices, eggs, bacon, sausage, pancakes, and real maple syrup graced the room at every table.

Eventually, we made our way back to the dock and began the labor of removing almost all of our gear to the dock to be rinsed with fresh water and dried in the sun. Items that had been hosed off and dried the previous day were set aside to remain dry. The boat was hosed off inside and out and left open to air-dry. By late afternoon, clean, dry gear was returned to a clean, dry boat. The boat was secured and back to town we went where we enjoyed the best meal of our trip at a little restaurant called the Impudent Oyster on a side street off the main thoroughfare (Route 6) near the center of town.

The morning again brought us bright sunshine and a repeat of the sumptuous breakfast of the day before. The harbormaster was going to have to wait.

Soon after arriving at the dock, midday, the dreaded harbormaster appeared before us once again.

"When will you be leaving?"

"We will sail with the tide," I replied. That response elicited a flood of the most valuable information of the trip.

"Be sure you sail against the incoming tide. The swells will not be breaking in the inlet. The current runs about six knots, so you will have to get out before it peaks or just after it peaks. Doesn't look like you can go that fast to me."

I thanked him profusely and assured him that I would not miss my window of opportunity. He turned and left.

We busied ourselves loading sandwiches, ice, and gas aboard the boat. Fishing boats came and went, none having to wait for a space to dock because of our presence. Several of the captains had heard of our odyssey and came over to talk to us about it. The captain of the boat we had passed seven miles out two days before made a special point of landing at the dock to introduce himself to us, examine our boat, and wish us well. A few of the men made mention of tropical storm Hannah heading north from the Carolinas. I was aware of the existence of the storm but had paid little attention to it being as far away as it was. When I turned on my VHF radio and tuned into the weather channels, I discovered the airwaves flooded with warnings about the storm headed our way and due to arrive within a day! Now I had to get serious.

While Lou completed preparations for leaving, I buried my nose in my Eldridge to estimate, as precisely as possible, the timing of peak currents in the inlet. I also discussed the timing of those currents with every captain I could talk to. We had to leave. Riding out the storm in Chatham Harbor was, for me, not an option, especially if the storm were to brake through the bar and reconfigure the entire harbor as storms had in the past. Although this was not advertised to be a particularly severe storm, I did not want to ride it out there. Provincetown was a secure and much better protected harbor. That's where I wanted to be when Hannah hit. The question was, would I be able to get there in time? There was a risk that the storm would overtake us at night as we were rounding Race Point at the tip of the Cape in that vast caldron of rip currents over a hundred square miles in area. Although not as dangerous as Pollock Rip, Race Point is no place to be caught in a storm, especially at night.

The wind was fresh and steady from the west-southwest at about fifteen knots gusting to twenty-five. The forecast called for moderate southwesterly breezes to continue throughout the rest of the day and into the evening. Currents were well into the flooding cycle and would peak around 3:00 p.m. in the cut. We had to leave as soon as we could. We prepared to sail with a reefed main and the storm jib. In the midst of these preparations, the harbormaster made a final visit.

"Understand you're headed for Provincetown."

"Yes, sir," I replied, thinking, where else would I be going since that is the only harbor within a fifty-mile range. That was simply how he chose to start the conversation.

"You can get around Race Point under the rip if you stay in close to land. Just hug the beach all the way around." Another pearl of wisdom that could be a dividing line between life and death. Again, I thanked him. He bid us good-bye and good luck and left.

Casting off, we left the safety of the dock for the cut through Chatham Bar to the open ocean. As we entered the central harbor area, the incoming current was about two knots against us. The sea was flowing through the narrow harbor to fill Pleasant Bay to the north. Lou raised the main with a single reef, reducing its exposed area by about a third. The storm jib went up next. We proceeded due south on a comfortable close reach. The harbor continued to narrow before opening up into the cut area where the slender barrier beach that formed the outer edge of the harbor ended and the shallow sandbar began. As the harbor narrowed, the speed of the current against us increased, soon approaching close to five knots. The combination of our full eight horsepower of "iron wind" and the stiff breeze barely moved us against the current toward the cut. We were less than an hour from peak current, which may have stopped us cold had we tarried any longer at the dock. Where the barrier beach ended, widening the area through which tidal water could move, the current slackened, allowing us to advance at an increased pace toward the little orange flags marking the cut. Seas in the cut were mild, as were the combers on either side. The incoming current was moving with the swells, thereby keeping them from steepening and breaking in the cut. Turning into the channel around the first orange flag, we picked up ground speed against the slowing current on our way to the freedom of open water.

Before we could complete what amounted to a U-turn from due south in the harbor to due north towards Provincetown in the open water, we would have to gradually turn downwind and beyond, jibing onto a port tack. We had been traveling due south in the harbor on a starboard reach (wind from starboard, sails set on the port side) with the wind from the west-southwest coming at us from the right side of the boat. As we turned left into the cut onto a southeastward heading, our new heading put us on a very broad reach and aligned with the channel (cut) through the bar. Upon clearing the bar and the little orange flags, we turned to the left again, jibing onto a port reach and headed north. Our U-turn was complete.

The race was on. Would we reach Provincetown before tropical storm Hannah? Conditions were ideal for making speed. *Yvaledon* was on a near-beam reach sailing north on a southwesterly wind. The current was with us and would remain so for several more hours. Seas were a gentle three to four feet. We could easily raise more sail and increase our speed made good by one- or two-tenths of a knot, but then we might have to reduce sail again, later, in stormy seas. We were already at hull speed, so I decided that a few tenths of a knot was insufficient advantage to risk having to reduce sail later in dangerous weather conditions at night. The engine was allowed to run to maintain battery charge while we sailed and to maximize our speed. I had started the engine by hand at the dock because the battery had inadequate charge to do the job. With the engine running, the electrical system was fully operational.

Hours passed as we made our way northward along the Cape's outer shore. The warm sun and easy breeze belied the dangerous storm racing to meet us around Race Point. Rapidly advancing storms do not cause a gradual deterioration of weather conditions. They strike suddenly with sharp wind gusts, rain squalls, and large waves. There is little or no time to run for shelter. Out where we were, there is no shelter.

While all was well, the time was right to break out the lunch: sandwiches, chips, water, V-8, apples, and a cookie for me. No meal is complete without desert. And just because we're out in the middle of the ocean in an eighteen-foot boat, that is no excuse not to have desert like a civilized human being. Lou thought that's a riot. He laughed the whole time I was eating my desert. Such a Neanderthal! We did agree on one important menu item—alcohol. There is a time and place for that, and this was neither.

As the sun set, we began to pick up navigational lights on shore. The GPS glowed with our orange course, which we followed slavishly. We also carefully followed our course on the chart in the event that our electrical system went dead, killing the GPS. The sun set before we reached Race Point, but we had made much better progress than I had originally planned. The preplanned GPS course took us well into the rip around Race Point. So I decided to stay on that course until I felt the effects of the rip current, at which time I would head toward shore to evade the rip as advised by Chatham's harbormaster.

I do not remember exactly when we hit the rip, but it was dark and we hit it like a wall. The boat started jumping up and down like a Mexican jumping bean. I immediately veered off to port toward shore and into calmer water. Unable to see the shoreline, I relied on the depth meter to guide us. I initially targeted a depth of fifty feet, but the bottom is so hilly I could not maintain that guideline. So I changed my criteria to a band of depth from twenty to fifty feet. That worked much better. By keeping the boat in water between twenty and fifty feet deep, I could maintain a fairly even course around the tip of the Cape, a safe distance from shore and out of the grip of the nasty rip.

The twenty-to-fifty-foot deep band of water pulled us disturbingly close to shore for a good stretch. We could only see the shoreline in dark relief against the lights of Provincetown, which gave us no visual depth perception at all but somehow seemed awfully close. The dark contour against the dim white background light revealed rolling sand dunes, occasional large rocks, scrub growth outcroppings, and infrequent shacks, or other structures. The sharp detail of the silhouettes bore witness to their close proximity. At 348 feet high, the brightly lit Pilgrim Monument was an omnipresent beacon from everywhere we went.

The tidal rise and fall of water at Provincetown is typically between nine and eleven feet. The sea sweeps around Race Point at impressive speeds as it fills and empties Cape Cod Bay, creating an expansive, deep water rip. The tip of Cape Cod curves around on itself in an ever tightening spiral, like the chambers of a nautilus. As we followed that spiral, we came ever closer into the wind, which had turned more westerly until we began to luff unable to turn farther. At that point we had to begin tacking upwind to make progress. The wind and current were against us. Progress became painfully slow. By the time we had to begin tacking, we had rounded Race Point into Cape Cod Bay. The rip was mostly behind us giving us an ever wider swath of calm water in which to sail. We could make long tacks without reentering the rip. Well after midnight we had come almost full circle onto a northeast heading into Provincetown's harbor at the core of the spiral.

By 2:00 a.m. we approached the breakwater at the entrance to the inner harbor. I could see nothing other than inky-black darkness beyond the breakwater but knew that the area was littered with moorings, boats, and a myriad of other unlit hazards sitting there, thinking at us, daring us to hit one of them. We would loiter outside the breakwater until dawn when we could see our way safely into port. I shut the engine down and heaved to, setting the sails and tiller to drive the boat at a snail's pace into the wind and current. Lou and I took turns resting on a seat while the other kept watch as we inevitably drifted off position. As necessary, we restarted the engine and repositioned the boat to drift once again. Thus, we planned to spend the night. Fat chance!

At 3:00 a.m., a few sprinkles of rain fell then stopped… minutes later another sprinkle. Hannah was upon us. Into our foul weather gear we climbed. By 3:30 a.m., the rain was steady and sharp wind gusts hit us without warning. By about four o'clock the sky had opened up with a torrential downpour and increasing winds that continued for the rest of the day and into the following night. Now we fought to keep on station outside the breakwater. The wind alternated between flat calm and sudden fifteen-to-twenty-knot gusts. The night was black. The only visible objects were the lights on the breakwater, a couple of buoys, and of course, the Pilgrim Monument. Lou was struck with a fatigue that he could no longer deny. Reclining on the port seat, he passed out, and for a full hour the man slept, face up in the driving rain as if in his own bed. When he awoke, he swore he had only slept for a few minutes. He got no argument from me. He had earned his claim.

Finally, jet-black faded to dark gray then to light gray. We could see the world around us. It wasn't pretty. We started the engine, manually, since the battery was no longer strong enough to do the job. We dropped and furled the main—the only sail that was still up—and into the harbor we went. The harbor was huge, nothing like I remembered it. I had no idea where to head, so I headed for the Pilgrim Monument. How's that for navigational brilliance? Except for the horrendous downpour, the air was clear and visibility was surprisingly good—no fog. The pouring rain and whipping wind turned the surface of the harbor into a froth that, in some cases, obliterated small objects from view, such as mooring buoys. Piers jutted out into the harbor as far as I could see in both directions. I headed for what appeared to be the largest grouping, hoping that would be the center of town and would have some small floating docks. The pilings supporting large piers are coated with tar and infested with crustaceans such as mussels and barnacles, which can shred the side of a boat in seconds. I did not want to have to tie up to one of those. Selecting the largest pier, about half a mile in length, I motored along its side perusing the scene. Multistory commercial buildings and billboards adorned its length. A roadway ran down the center for the entire length of the pier between the buildings. Open ocean fishing vessels, dredges, and other workboats were tied up here and there. I saw no tankers or freighters on that pier. A long floating dock appeared with dozens of slips, most of which were empty. A gangplank at least 150 feet in length ascended from the dock to the top of the pier about twenty-five feet above the water. At the bottom of the gangplank was an empty slip that looked perfect for an eighteen-foot sailboat. And at six thirty in the morning in the pouring rain, who was going to object?

After tying the boat up with bow and stern lines, which limit the freedom of movement sideways, and fore and aft spring lines, which limit the boat's movement frontward and backward, we gathered our things to go ashore. In the process, the inside of the boat got quite wet. There was simply no way to prevent that in such foul weather. At least it was fresh water and not salt, so it would eventually dry.

Up the long gangplank we trudged, weighed down by our bags of shore gear and our equally oppressive burden of fatigue. At the top we passed through a great wooden arch sheltering two large ice-making machines on the left and a Coke machine on the right. A small storage area appeared next to the ice machines. No one was around. After passing through the arch onto the pier's central roadway, we could see no sign of humanity in either direction. We headed on foot toward town. *Yvaledon* seemed so small in her slip. The top of her thirty-foot mast was at about eye level from our elevated vantage on the pier. On we went. I could soon smell the town, a foul mix of garbage and grill grease. This was not the quaint little village of my youth. At the end of the pier was a large square where major docks, including ferry docks, merged in a frenzy of small shops, parking areas, transportation, and public service facilities. Past all this ran the main drag, State Route 6, or Main Street in this area. Rising above it all on the highest hill sat the Pilgrim Monument. At about a mile distant, it was still an imposing presence.

Food—we needed to eat! The closest place open at that early hour would do. A small café advertised breakfast to our left. In we went. What a blessed relief to be in somewhere and out of the rain! Almost instantly, overheating in the warm humid air inside the café, we peeled off our outer weather gear and sat down. A waiter came over and offered us OJ and coffee to which we wasted no time in approving. There we sat with our menus, and our drinks, again staring blankly as our bodies absorbed the energy. A few more men entered the café. One came over to the man seated near us and gave him a kiss on top of his head. Oh, yes, we were in Provincetown. More gestures of warmth and acceptance ensued as we sat and didn't look. When a couple and their two kids came in and ordered breakfast, I felt a little more comfortable. Our breakfast of eggs and bacon, toast, and home fries was nourishing; but that is as far as I can go with the credits. Finally energized with food and drink, we exited the café back onto the street and into the rain. Now to find a place to stay. I had noted a small Chamber of Commerce kiosk near the end of our pier on the way in.

Upon entering the kiosk, we were immediately confronted by a portly young lady seated in a wheelchair behind a desk. She greeted us with a warm smile and cheery, "Hello! Can I help you?"

"Why, yes," I replied. "We are looking for a place to stay."

She let out a sudden laugh that was so loud it must have been heard to the end of our pier. Without bothering to notice my shock, she began shuffling through the morning's status reports of current vacancies. She began with lower-end offerings.

Seeing our lack of enthusiasm, she moved on to more upscale accommodations. The Black Pearl, she noted, was a real fine property, not too far away, with a vacancy. That sounded as good as anything discussed so far. She called the owner to see if it was still available. It was. We decided to take a look. Armed with directions, we headed for the door.

"Stop, wait…He's going to come over here and pick you up. He says the weather's too bad to walk." She hung up the phone.

"But we didn't agree to stay there. We are just going to look at it."

"He knows that, but he doesn't care. He says he doesn't want you walking to his place in the rain." Again, she broke out into a stentorian laugh, louder than the first.

Within minutes, we were in his car headed for the Black Pearl. Past a myriad of small shops, we turned left onto a narrow street, continuing past more shops and private residences with tiny front yards, a few filled with a single dumpster that took up the entire yard, we soon arrived at the Black Pearl in what appeared to be a relatively nice area. Once inside, we arranged to stay two nights. Our host showed us to our suite on the third floor overlooking much of the town. Ceilings sloped in every direction to accommodate the exterior roof configuration. We had a private entrance leading to an external wooden stairway that descended past the first two floors to ground level. The man's home was modest but very comfortable. He had made every effort to make the place as attractive and inviting as he could afford. Our rooms were very clean.

Once we had secured a place to stay, I wanted to return to the boat to make sure it was properly secured and riding out the storm without being damaged against the slip. I also wanted to retrieve additional things we would need for our stay ashore and that may need drying out in our rooms. Descending the internal staircase, we landed in our host's kitchen and living area. He introduced us to his partner and insisted on taking us back to the pier so we would not have to walk back in the rain. He was truly a good man.

Our host drove us out onto the pier to the arch leading down to our boat. As we exited the car, the wind-whipped rain pelted us unmercifully. Vaguely aware of a large human form standing in the archway, we hurried in that direction toward the gangplank leading down to the floating dock. As we approached, the form moved into our path making clear his intent to stop us. Under the semi-shelter of the arch, I could see his face glaring at me from under the hood of his yellow, commercial grade, rubber foul weather jacket. He was wearing khaki shorts revealing heavily scarred, well-tanned legs, and leather work boots. With rain cascading off his foul weather gear, he conveyed an ominous intent. I came to a stop about four feet from him, Lou behind me.

"Do you two belong to that little sailboat down there?"

I responded with a firm, "Yes."

"Do you make a habit of helping yourselves to other people's slips?"

I stood there dumfounded, staring up into that hard craggy face, not knowing how to respond to the question.

"You come in here, plunk yourselves down in someone else's slip, then disappear without saying a word to anybody. Get your boat off my dock! I don't care where you go, but get it out of here."

My mind was racing. The hostility was beyond the crime. Why was he so angry? We could have easily moved the boat into any of the other empty slips. And we had returned. Then I became aware of how we must have looked to him, standing there in our matching and colorful Helly Hansen foul weather suits. In almost any other port, we could have looked like members of a sailing team but not in this one. He did not look like the kind of man who would take kindly to a couple of gay guys arriving on a sailboat and sneaking into one of his slips. Based on that assumption, I found my tongue.

"We have traveled a long way, and the ocean ate our dinghy in rough seas off Chatham a few days ago. We have been under way for over two weeks in that little boat. We are exhausted and hungry. We did not mean to take anybody's slip. We are just looking for shelter from the storm."

Apparently unfazed by my plea, the old goat continued on, "You did everything all wrong. You came in here and tied up to someone else's slip, didn't bother to look for the dock master, then just disappeared. Where are you going now to get your things and disappear again for the rest of the day?" I dared not admit that's exactly what I planned to do. "Get your boat off my dock, or I'll have it impounded by the coast guard," he continued, becoming angrier as he spoke.

"When we came in, there was no one around anywhere."

"There's always someone on duty! You never checked the office!" I glanced in the direction of the "storage area."

Again, I dared not admit that I mistook his office for a storage area.

Now in a panic, I stammered, "Where can I go?"

"That's your problem. Just get your boat off my dock! You did everything all wrong. Haven't you ever been in a boatyard before?"

Now backed into a corner, I said, "Where is the coast guard office?"

"It's over on the next dock," he proclaimed, pointing in the general direction. "What do you want to know that for?"

"I want to explain our situation and ask them for some help and advice about what we can do." To make matters worse, I noticed my ride slowly leaving the area. My host from the Black Pearl, noting the trouble we were in, had decided that this was going to take a while to resolve, and that he could no longer stay and wait.

The loud, angry voice to my right jolted my attention back to the business at hand, "That ain't goin' to help you. All they're goin' to do is call me and you're right back where you started." With that, he turned his back and headed into the "storage area" that was indeed his office. I followed him inside. The office was fairly large as it expanded around and behind the ice machines. He walked around a small counter to the right and seated himself behind a large wooden desk. In the open area to the left were two smaller desks, one of which was occupied be another man, obviously his "staff." As the dock master removed his foul weather jacket, I saw his hands, grotesquely gnarled and missing most of their fingers, apparently injured in the same accident that severely scarred his legs. That gave him an even harder, coldly dispassionate appearance that, under the circumstances, made our predicament seem even more hopeless than it had before.

Stalling for time, I mumbled something about sailing all night into Butler Hole, and twelve to fifteen foot seas in Pollock Rip, searching for an opening in the combers across Chatham Bar, getting caught in a rogue wave that ripped my dinghy off the back of the boat…on I babbled…about how exhausted we were. I began to feel about as pathetic as I must have sounded as I contemplated the agony of going back out into that storm to search for another place to stop and tie up.

"Where did you start from?" he interrupted.

"Noank, Connecticut a few weeks ago, near Mystic."

I pressed on, "There are a lot of empty slips down there," referring to the long floating dock some 25 feet below the pier. "Would you be good enough to rent us one of them?"

"That'll be one hundred dollars a night." Then in a moment of unexpected integrity and with an apparent twinge of guilt, he added, "That's the same as I would charge anyone, not just you. That's the going rate for a slip here." I instantly believed him, having recently shelled out sixty dollars a night in Nantucket for a mooring half a mile off shore.

"I'll take it for two nights." As I reached into my left rear pocket for my wallet, I saw Lou moving forward with his credit card saying, "Here, take this." Lou's face was ashen white. The poor man, clearly traumatized by the exchange between me and the dock master, wanted only peace. Lou is one of the gentlest people I have ever met. Even the hint of discord normally alarms him. This trip was becoming an adventure beyond his wildest dreams. The dock master took the credit card and processed it for two hundred dollars. He then assigned us a slip other than the one we were in.

We left the office and descended the long ramp to the floating dock. The rain and wind were debilitating and relentless. Every small task seemed a struggle. The thought of moving the boat in those conditions was daunting but on with it was the only way forward. I bent over and removed one of the spring lines from its cleat. I then laboriously removed the stern line from its cleat. Exhaustion was becoming overwhelming. Then I saw the dock master at the top of the gangplank heading down. This could not be good. What now? Wind whipped rain lashed his foul weather gear pushing him off balance and forcing him to grab the hand rail for stability. Lou and I just stood there and watched as the wretched man traversed the long incline and stood before us ready to speak.

"I have a deal for you. I'm going to put you on a mooring."

I instantly flared. "I can't take a mooring. I have no dinghy!"

I'm not sure if I just thought that or if I actually said it, but he continued, "You can use my dinghy," pointing to a decrepit little pram sitting turtle on the dock at our feet. I had not even noticed it. Before I could ask "How much is that going to cost?" he said, "Cost you nothing. The dinghy's on me. That's my personal dinghy. I never processed the MasterCard. I tore it up." Silence, nobody spoke. I was so tired I actually thought to myself that it would be worth two hundred dollars to take the slip and not have to take the boat a quarter of a mile around the end of the pier to a mooring and then row the dinghy, who knows how far, back to the dock. Could I even row against the weather in that little box and would the waves swamp it before we reached the dock? Breaking the silence, the dock master went on, cracking a sheepish smile. "From one old salt to another, I know what you're doing. You're just trying to survive. I've done that before myself." The peace pipe had been stoked and drafted and handed to me. I accepted the pipe and took my draft by accepting his offer. He smiled broadly, and we chatted for several minutes exchanging nautical war stories. Finally, he left feeling relieved of his guilt, and we, feeling equally relieved, but for different reasons also left for our assigned mooring, dinghy in tow.

As we ventured forth into the storm, wind-driven water streamed from every fitting on the deck, vanishing overboard into the sea. Rounding the end of the pier, we quickly found our mooring amazingly close to the pier and even closer to the dinghy dock at its base. The one-hundred-foot row from the mooring to the dinghy dock was going to be a "breeze" even in that storm. We secured *Yvaledon*, rowed to the dock, and got out crawling up onto the floating dock on our hands and knees. Standing on the edge of the dock, I gave a tug on the painter to ease the craft up and out of the water. The little wooden pram increased its weight defiantly trying hatefully, or so it seemed, to weigh as much as it possibly could—ideally simulating the heft of a fully loaded barge—as we hauled it out of the water onto the low dock. We rolled it over onto its gunwales and secured the dinghy so it wouldn't blow away in the storm. With lead in our shoes, we headed back to the dock master's office on foot to confirm that we had found the mooring and had secured the man's dinghy safely on the dock.

While in the office a call came in that our host from the Black Pearl was coming to retrieve us. Finally, safe, dry, and semisettled in our room at the Black Pearl, we luxuriated in one of the best hot showers we had ever had. Funny how a warm, wet shower can feel so good after a long wet sail. One would think that a dry, hot sauna would be more appealing, but no, it is not. The clean factor of a shower is irreplaceable. While Lou showered, I unpacked and vice versa. The two rooms became strewn with our wet clothing and gear hanging from every hook and lamp and other suitable furnishing to dry.

Reenergized by the showers and clean, dry clothes, and with a surfeit of adrenaline still coursing through our veins, Lou and I headed back out into the storm. Clad once again in our foul weather gear, we set out to find a gin mill and some good food. Stopping at a sidewalk café, we were seated in a glassed-in area right next to the sidewalk where we could look up and down the street and watch people, cars, and bicycles go by. After all we had been through, that scene had a strange calming, even salubrious effect on the two of us. After one or two libations to calm the jangled nerves of two still very hyper sailors, a wonderful seafood dinner was served and savored. This was followed, of course, by desert for me, to the demented entertainment of my barbarian traveling companion.

We were greeted the next day by a warm sun, dry weather, and a gentle breeze—a perfect ten! No sailing for us. We were going to enjoy Provincetown. After jumping out of bed to rush to breakfast before noon, we found a most delightful place with a second story deck overhanging the sidewalk, and decorated with flowers and plants, that was still serving breakfast. Our kind of place!

Onward and upward! All the way to the top of the Pilgrim Monument, step by step we climbed the hundreds of stone slabs leading up the dimly lit, dank, spiral stairway to the top of the solid, granite structure. Along the way we took breaks to peer out of the small barred windows to see our little boat swinging at its mooring. Each time we looked from progressively higher vantages, the boat appeared notably smaller than from the previous look. At the top we could hardly see the boat, but the view was spectacular! We were high enough to see the entire contour of Provincetown, Race Point, and the sea beyond. We could see the docks, sand dunes, streets, and buildings, and Route

6 disappearing into the distance along the sandy arm of the Cape. Although calm at the base, the wind blew a constant twenty knots or more at the top.

Having completed our climb up and down the Pilgrim Monument, Lou and I were wandering about in the museum at its base. There in the center of a large room was a model of a typical fishing weir identical to the one I came to know so intimately a lifetime ago. I showed Lou where and how I managed to sail into the thing and how I sailed out.

CHAPTER XIII

SUDDEN DEATH
OF THE TWENTY-FIRST CENTURY

The next morning we set out for Wellfleet along the eastern shore of Cape Cod Bay. The sail was delightful and uncharacteristically uneventful. As a result, I hardly remember any of it in detail except that Lou and I loved every minute of that peaceful passage. I do remember that we were followed at length by a Cape Cod style catboat that could not overtake us despite being on a broad reach—a strong advantage for the gaff-rigged craft. As we sailed the long way around a reef to enter the channel into Wellfleet, the cat cut across the reef and, to my chagrin, beat us in by at least a half hour. After docking at the local marina, the catboat sailor came over to see us and, after some conversation, admitted that he "bounced over a few shallow spots" and had to pull his centerboard up to keep moving. I then felt a little less wussy about my more conservative track. While we talked, several other couples from nearby boats approached, intrigued by our distinctive boat and its distant hail port of "Noank." Lou and I regaled them with tales of our adventures to their obvious delight. The dock attendant seemed to be equally captivated. Taking advantage of the assembled local knowledge, we asked our usual questions about walk-to eateries and inns. We were directed to the "Bookstore" restaurant past the parking lot and across the street and to some vague places to stay, "up the road in that direction," as indicated by arms pointing toward town. The boat was tidy and tucked away in its assigned spot at the dock; our curious friends began melting away back to their own boats, so we eventually wandered off in search of the "Bookstore." After dinner at the Bookstore & Restaurant Seafood Grill and our customary celebratory wine—each leg of our trip had to be celebrated appropriately, some legs more, shall we say, "enthusiastically"? than others since no alcohol was consumed enroute—we walked blindly along the shore road as directed to who-knows-where. Soon a large house with a lighted sign appeared within sight of the beach. The entire house was fronted by a long, screened-in porch with two doors into the residence. At the far end of the porch, the top half of a Dutch door stood open to a small office. Inside, a man was beckoning us to approach. We arranged to stay the night and were ushered to a small outbuilding alongside the main structure where we were to encamp in a ground level room. The accommodation was plain but adequate. Most importantly, it was clean.

In the morning, as we were on the dock preparing to leave for Barnstable, we became engaged in conversation with the dock master who had heard all about our trip via the dock grapevine that must have started with the attendant from the night before. So impressed was he with our endeavor, from how far away we had come and how we had gotten there in our small sailboat, that he waived the usual ten-dollar berthing fee.

A stiff breeze induced us to bend on the storm jib and to take a reef in the main. We had had enough excitement the previous two weeks and were looking forward to a relatively relaxing sail to Barnstable. We backed out of our spot at the end of the dock and waived good-bye to our new friends. Clearing the long channel back into the bay, we set our sails for Barnstable on the southern shore of Cape Cod Bay.

Storm clouds gathered once again. We watched the approaching squall line close in from our starboard quarter. This looked to be a wild but probably short ride since we could see clear sky all around the disturbance. By all appearances, the storm could be intense while it lasted. We donned our foul weather suits in preparation for the meteorological festivities. Now that we were committed to another nautical challenge and psyched up, once again, for the inescapable thrill of the "chased," I was hoping that this would be a ten-to-twenty-minute, thrill-packed, sixty-knot wind event like the one I had experienced over forty years ago in a thunder squall onboard the *Rosa II.*

Alas, I was disappointed. The wind kicked up to only about twenty-five knots and hit gradually, but the rain was like a tropical downpour flattening out the seas with its intensity. The storm lasted for over forty minutes then gradually diminished trailing clear sky and bright sunshine. We shook out the reef in the main and glided over the silvery sea into the warming light of the sun.

Easing into tiny Barnstable Harbor, we docked at the Millway Marina and found our way to the Mattakeese Wharf restaurant adjacent to the marina. There seemed to be no place to stay close to the marina, so we decided to have dinner at the restaurant before it closed and deal with the accommodation part of our dilemma later. As we dined, darkness fell and the weather closed in. The staff at the restaurant began making phone calls on our behalf to help us find lodgings. One gentleman, from the Ashley Manor over a mile away, offered to drive over in the pouring rain and pick us up to stay at his inn. The hour was late, but he arrived in a van and retrieved us as promised. Traveling for long minutes through the blinding rain with no sense of direction and what seemed to be miles of turning, twisting, and climbing, the grand Victorian structure loomed startlingly like a castle perched high on a grassy knoll, the entire estate ringed by an equally imposing black iron fence. Our van entered the open gate and climbed the steep drive to the manor. The bright lights illuminating the exterior highlighted the driving rain cascading off the roof and other architectural features. One could imagine scenes from an Alfred Hitchcock or Sherlock Holmes tale unfolding within. However, once inside, we were warmly welcomed by his wife and shown to our suite. The couple bid us good night and left us alone to settle in. On the morn, greeted once again by warm sunshine, we were treated to a splendid homemade breakfast by the inn's proprietors on their picturesque rear patio. We were getting kind of used to this relatively easy sailing life in Cape Cod Bay. However, a more pungent form of reality lay in wait but a few leagues away.

We departed Barnstable Harbor with a smart southwest breeze heading for the Cape Cod Canal. Beginning with a close reach, and eventually hardening to windward, we entered the canal late morning. The current ran with us, but the wind was right in our teeth, forcing us to drop sail and motor. The electrical system had become an increasing problem. The knot meter and depth sounder would cut out without warning followed shortly thereafter by the GPS thus requiring the use of the engine to recharge the battery. Of course, with insufficient juice to power the electronics, the engine had to be started by hand. Somewhere in the canal the entire electrical system went totally dead—nothing electrical worked, including the fuel gage. Dipping the tank with a stick to measure the fuel level was impossible due to the serpentine fill pipe. Night sailing would also be prohibited with no running lights and no compass light. An unplanned stop at Cape Cod Shipbuilding in Wareham, Massachusetts, on Buzzards Bay at the other end of the canal would be required to investigate and repair the system. In the meantime, getting through the canal was the immediate order of business.

The current in the canal peaks at upwards of 4.5 knots. We were moving through the water at a little more than five knots at three-fourth throttle. Full throttle would have given us a bit more speed but consumed much more fuel. Our speed through the water, combined with the swift current, hustled us along at almost ten knots over the ground as we flew through the canal. The land cut portion of the canal opens into Buzzards Bay via Hog Island Channel at the western end. The wind was funneling into that end of the canal with a vengeance. At least a dozen large sailing yachts were struggling against the elements when we approached Hog Island Channel from the land cut. Boats were hobby-horsing in the steep rip seas. The seas had been building in essentially unlimited fetch from the open ocean through Buzzards Bay into Hog Island Channel. There they met with the tidal current coming the other way from the land cut. The swift current charging at the incoming waves steepened them into five-to-six-foot monsters. Rip seas in a current that strong become almost like vertical walls of water—similar to standing waves in a river (rapids) where the water passes over large rocks, but these were much larger than river rapids. A thirty-foot blue-water ketch in front of us was pitching so wildly in the seas that, when upended in the bow, we could see her entire deck as if from an airplane. When she dove back down into a trough, her canoe stern came out of the water exposing a third of her bottom and the prop, which spun uselessly in the air until plunged back down into the sea. Her prop was spending so much time airborne, that we gradually passed her powered only by our little eight horsepower Yamaha. A long, sleek, seventy-foot racing yacht slid past everybody, cutting through the seas like an oversized stiletto.

Not wanting to arrive at Cape Cod Shipbuilding late in the day, we headed into the narrow but protected channel leading to Onset. After docking at the Point Independence Yacht Club, we spent a pleasant evening in Onset and stayed the night at an ocean side inn. Before leaving in the morning, I filled the fuel tank.

We motored down the narrow mile-and-a-half-long channel from Onset to Hog Island Channel, set sail, and headed southwest and then north for the ten-mile run into Cape Cod Shipbuilding at the head of the short Wareham River. Hog Island Channel was a pussycat compared to the day before.

Mr. Goodwin, president of CCS, was there to greet us when we arrived. A tall, handsome man well into his seventies or early eighties with a full head of white hair, he came aboard with Andy, his chief carpenter and master technician. Together they tore into the electrical system while Lou and I stood by on the slip to answer any questions they might have. After about two hours of working in the cramped quarters of the small cuddy cabin, they had the system running perfectly but had not found the root cause of the electrical system failure. The close of business was drawing nigh, so there was nothing more they could do that day. Since the system seemed to be fully functional, I decided not to delay our trip any longer and to leave the next morning. While we cleaned up the boat, taking advantage of the fresh water hose on the slip, the shops and office closed down. Everyone left, the last person locking the gate behind. We were given the combination to the lock so that we could get out and go into town to find a place to eat and stay.

The next day was sunny and pleasant. We cast off and headed downstream toward Buzzards Bay. Five minutes out of the slip, the electrical system died for good. We decided to continue on. We would sail by basic means, the old-fashioned way, relying on our paper charts, tidal current data in Eldridge, compass, dividers, protractor, binoculars, and the hand bearing (hockey puck) compass. We would have to avoid night sailing since all running lights were nonfunctional. I estimated that we were three days out of Noank, our final destination. The longest leg would be a thirty-five-mile expanse of open water from Cuttyhunk across Rhode Island Sound to Block Island. That distance would have to be covered in the available fourteen hours of daylight. We would also have to wait for agreeable weather which meant, primarily, a fair and strong wind. If we lost the wind, we would motor to maintain speed. Gassing up in Cuttyhunk was part of the plan.

Isn't it amazing how quickly a modern day sailing vessel, bristling with twenty-first-century electronics, can be set back to early twentieth-century standards of navigation and operation? No one should ever wander very far from home port without basic navigation tools and a solid and comfortable grasp of basic navigation techniques.

Our twenty-five-mile course from the mouth of the Wareham River to Cuttyhunk, at the southeastern tip of the Elizabeth Island chain, was to take us diagonally across Buzzards Bay in a southwesterly direction. The favorable west wind would probably turn toward the southwest later in the day forcing us off our intended route. That being the case, we would motor into the wind to maintain course and schedule to arrive in Cuttyhunk before dark. A slight tidal current of less than a half knot would persist against us all afternoon increasing our risk of having to motor to maintain course. A number of large navigation buoys strategically placed along the way would serve us well as we progressed.

A weak tidal current in the bay gave us a slight lift westward during the morning hours through about 1:00 p.m. For full advantage of the westward drift, I kept *Yvaledon* hard on the wind on a starboard tack. After that, the adverse eastward flow of the incoming tide, coupled with a breeze settling in from the southwest, began forcing us east of our goal. By midafternoon, the engine was cranked up to enable the necessary course correction. The sails stayed up as long as they contributed to our forward motion, which they did for several more hours even as they luffed softly along their forward edges. Eventually, the wind headed us to the extent that the sails had to come down. By then we were closing in on Cuttyhunk.

Inside the quiet, sheltered harbor, the dock master directed us to the dinghy dock to tie up for the night. Quite insulted by the implication that *Yvaledon* was no more than a dinghy, I headed around the main dock to the dinghy dock and tied up.

Hoping not to have to sleep aboard, either in the cramped cabin or in the salty cockpit, we headed out on foot to find the Cuttyhunk Fishing Club, one of the few places left on the island, mid-September, not closed for the season. After a mile hike, we walked into the club looking for the proprietor. A helpful guest informed us that no one of authority was on the premises. The guests, at that point, were on their own. Any problems they may have encountered would have to be dealt with unassisted by management. We called a number left for the guests to use in an emergency only to be confronted with a canned message of no value whatsoever. The helpful guest directed us to another inn high on a hill within sight of the Fishing Club. Off we went.

Arriving at the Avalon atop the hill, we entered the lobby/ activity room only to see a crowd of teenagers energetically moving about, alternately carrying on animated conversation inside the lobby and playing soccer outside on the lawn. Finally, we asked one of them for a proprietor. The lad responded that one was around, but he did not know where. If we just waited for a while, he would show up. Given that helpful advice, we sat down on a luxurious leather sofa and waited and watched. Eventually, after about forty minutes, the man showed up. We told him of our plight and asked for accommodations for the night. He offered us a room that was not set up, but if we waited, he would have one of the boys prepare it for us. He had a deal. Another ten minutes and we followed him to a building in the rambling complex where our room awaited. The room was clean, but the smell of mildew was suffocating. Fortunately, neither Lou nor I are allergic to mildew. However, the smell was so intense that we knew we would find it hard to sleep.

We decided to return to the boat and set it up to sleep, even though we had paid for the room. Arriving at our dinghy dock shortly before dark, we had barely started to settle in when a couple came along the dock to use their dinghy. They, of course, stopped to talk to us before moving on. We realized there would be no privacy on that dock, especially in the morning when the place became more active. So back to the inn on the hill we headed. A small kiosk on the main dock attracted our attention. Someone seemed to be inside, and the window was open as if for business. A sign advertised fresh seafood. Hungry enough to eat worms, we ventured over to seek our culinary fortune. The lady behind the counter offered hot clam chowder and raw oysters on the half shell. Sold! Seeing no place to sit and eat, we sat down on the dock and devoured some of the freshest seafood on the planet. Unfortunately, the portions were very small, leaving us still hungry. Darkness was setting in. We hurried to finish eating so that we could continue our trek back to the Avalon. Our hike took us along paved streets, through peoples' backyards and through woods by flashlight, the only way that we had been directed to get to the place and assured by friendly residents we met along the way that most people on foot use that route.

After hot and badly needed showers, we retired to our beds. The mildew problem was as bad as we expected. Unable to sleep, we wandered the grounds arriving at a large kitchen and dining area buzzing with teen activity. The girls had set up a long table creatively and, I might say, lavishly decorated with linen napkins and other materials scavenged from the surrounding facility. Lou and I were both impressed. Spotting the proprietor, who apparently was also functioning as a chaperone, we asked him about food for ourselves. He generously offered us access to his food and kitchen facilities, toured us through the freezer and fridge, cupboards, and other storage areas. Then he set up an outdoor grill for us to use. After lighting the grill, he left us to our own devices. We went to work in the kitchen alongside the teenagers, who seemed more amused by the presence of two old men than annoyed. They talked with us like we were part of their group as we worked together preparing our own separate meals—at ten o'clock at night. Not wanting to further impose on the friendly youngsters, Lou and I wound up enjoying our delicious burgers with chips, pickles, and coffee in the dark by the light of the moon on the back of a golf cart next to the kitchen. Tourist accommodations on the tiny island are limited, especially off-season.

Feeling much better, Lou and I returned to our quarters and, tired enough to ignore the mildew, fell asleep.

Sleep was fitful at best. Morning came and we returned to the boat. Concerned about the quantity of fuel left in the tank, I inquired with the dock master as to a source for gasoline. We were shocked to learn that there were no gas stations on the island.

"I have seen people driving around in cars on the island. Where are they getting their gas?" I inquired.

"People bring their own fuel from the mainland for the few cars requiring it. Most folks use golf carts to get around."

"Well, what about the boats? Where do they gas up?"

"See that Coast Guard station over there?" The large white block letters were visible from anywhere in the harbor. "That's not a Coast Guard station anymore. It's the gas dock. The old guy that runs it opens for business only once a day, usually in the morning sometime between eight and twelve o'clock. It's different every day—depends on his mood."

"Can we call him and ask him to come down early today?" I pressed.

"I wouldn't do that if I were you," came the reply. "He doesn't care much to be rousted out of bed this early in the morning. He might just refuse to come down at all. You'll know when he's there. He raises a little flag on that pole by the dock there."

Now I had a critical decision to make. Do we wait to gas up and lose precious daylight for the long passage to Block Island, or do we leave immediately with the unknown quantity of fuel that we have? We also faced the added risk of an adverse westerly wind later in the day slowing us down and forcing more extensive use of the engine, thus increasing the likelihood of running out of fuel before reaching Block. This, in turn, could force us into the night without running lights or a compass light. We did have flashlights aboard and a beam light to signal oncoming vessels at night to, hopefully, avoid collision.

A strong easterly wind was already blowing as part of an advancing frontal system. Chances were that it would continue for most of the day at least. With prevailing winds normally blowing from the southwest at that time of year, we would likely not get a better breeze to whisk us on our way westward toward Block than the one we had that very morning. After a brief discussion with Lou, we agreed to set sail and head out to sea.

A large nun buoy marked our point of departure from Cuttyhunk. I set a course of 265 degrees to Block Island, some thirty-five nautical miles distant. As we left the nun buoy behind, I continually took back-azimuth readings to the buoy with my hand bearing compass to keep the buoy on the reciprocal heading of eighty-five degrees (265 minus 180) thus assuring a course of 265 degrees. The boat's compass heading had to be set a few degrees higher than the desired course in order to maintain the eighty-five-degree back-azimuth to the nun buoy and the corresponding 265 degree course to Block, probably due to a slight offsetting tidal current. When the nun buoy could no longer be seen in the distance, even with binoculars, I maintained the boat's heading and hoped for the best. Our next and only reference was a whistle buoy about twenty-five miles ahead. If we stayed on course, we would pass the buoy about a mile to starboard.

Progress was good at slightly over four knots. During the early afternoon, clear skies became cloudy and visibility was reduced in a warm haze of increasing humidity. The breeze was turning to the south, putting us on a beam reach. That was great for speed, but if the wind continued turning toward the southwest, we would be forced away from Block. Meanwhile, we kept our eyes peeled for the whistle buoy to starboard, where we expected it to appear, as well as to port where we did not expect to see it. If we were to see it at all in the haze, we would see it when directly abeam and closest to the boat.

The wind continued to shift westward, placing us on a close reach and slowing our speed forward. The whistle buoy came into view only about a half mile to starboard. I had overcorrected somewhat and was one-half mile north of my desired 265 degree course line. To correct my heading and get back on course to our target, green bell off Block Island's North Point, I would have to turn approximately ten degrees into the wind. When I did that, the sails began to luff. The engine had to be started with nearly ten miles to go to enter Great Salt Pond, Block Island's main harbor. Again, we were able to motor-sail.

Finally, we could see the green bell off Block Island's North Point marking the deep end of Block Island North Reef, which rises gradually over about a mile and a half from the buoy to the beach on North Point. The wind had continued to turn westward rendering the sails totally useless. Wind speed had increased as it turned into our faces, and the seas were chopping up over the reef. It was time to take the sails down. That was a teachable moment. Lou had not taken the main down in rough conditions like those. There was a golden opportunity—rough but not extreme. I offered Lou the chance, and like the sturdy New Englander he is, he jumped at it. For the next half hour, I watched and coached the seventy-three-year-old man as he struggled with a violent sail in four-to-five-foot seas. Lou often stumbled and slipped on slick surfaces, including the sail itself as he took the sail down, furled it into a tight roll on the boom, and secured everything properly for a yacht-like entry into Great Salt Pond. Regardless of our struggles, I try never to enter any harbor looking like a disheveled rag-bagger. Lou had taken one more successful and giant leap toward becoming a skilled and seasoned sailor. He had learned more in one season than many people learn in a lifetime of casual and uninstructed sailing.

I could see a buoy about twenty degrees off to port in the haze and assumed it was the green bell off North Point that we were still near. Setting a heading of 208 degrees to skirt the northwestern coast of Block toward the harbor entrance to Great Salt Pond, I could see land faintly in the haze past the buoy, directly in front of us, and even to starboard. That was not right. I should see only open water dead ahead and to starboard. I slowed the engine and checked Eldridge for the current flow around Block at that time of day. My suspicions were confirmed. In my undistracted focus on Lou as he furled the mainsail, I never noticed that we had washed over North Reef onto its eastern side. The buoy that I saw in the haze off to port was not the green bell I thought it to be but instead was a local can buoy off Old Britton Rock in three feet of water on Block's northeastern shore!

I had made a potentially serious navigational error that, aside from the obvious risk, would cost us unnecessary spent fuel to correct and reposition ourselves back onto the west side of North Reef so that we could begin the 3.5 mile leg along Block's northwestern shore toward the harbor entrance to Great Salt Pond. Luckily, after motoring northwest to retrace our "steps," we sighted the "real" North Point bell buoy within about fifteen minutes. We had not drifted as far afield as I had feared. With daylight waning and visibility reduced in the haze, I approached the buoy closely enough to make a positive identification of its marking, "1BI." From there I set a heading of 208 degrees to the entrance to Great Salt Pond. We crossed our fingers hoping that we still had enough fuel to make it all the way in. As we left the green bell in our wake, Lou ran repeated back-azimuths to the buoy to keep us on the twenty-eight-degree reverse course line and the 208-degree course line for as long as we could see the buoy. We only had to travel a few miles without a specific navigational reference, such as a buoy or a land based beacon, before spotting the well-marked harbor entrance. This was no time to run out of fuel!

Had we run out of fuel and the engine died, and with no electricity to power the GPS, night navigation (running) lights, compass light, VHF radio, depth sounder, and other "essentials" of modern boating, how would we have managed safely? Even if the engine kept running but darkness set in before we reached Block Island, we would still be without electricity, so the same question can be asked. Let's take the worst-case scenario in which the engine dies. First, we would raise the mainsail and jib to give ourselves propulsion. Due to the direction of the wind, we would be forced to sail off on a port tack at an angle away from Block Island and the harbor entrance. We would mark our present (starting) position and time of day with a pencil on the chart. We would estimate our speed and direction, taking into account any effect of current and draw a line on the chart in the direction of estimated travel. At the point on the chart that we felt we could come about and head directly for the harbor entrance, we would make a mark. Dividing the distance between the two marks by our estimated speed would yield the elapsed time and time of day that we should come about onto the starboard tack and head for the harbor entrance.

As darkness set in, we would begin to see harbor entrance lights, which we could use to establish actual position unless, or course, the haze had turned into a dense fog and the lights on the entrance jetty could not penetrate far enough to be seen from where we were. Again, let's assume the worst—a foggy night. Being seen by local traffic would be a top priority. A radar reflector was already up. We had a handheld VHF radio that we could use to alert area boaters of our presence, location, and heading and that we were visually dark with no functioning running lights. We would use a handheld flashlight or beam light to illuminate the sails and sweep the horizon every few minutes to make ourselves periodically visible. We would sound a horn at frequent intervals, as required by law for vessels in the fog under power or sail—the signals are different for sail and power—depending on our mode of propulsion. With all these precautions in play, we would still listen for the sound of approaching engines and pray that no one smacked into us.

Once within visual range of the harbor entrance light beacon on the jetty, and/or within earshot of the horn on the jetty beacon or the clanging of nearby bell buoy, we would make our way into the harbor and anchor under sail in any open area just off the main channel. If the wind were brisk, I would reef or double reef the main just to keep the boat speed down inside the harbor.

The importance of having backup paper charts and basic navigation tools aboard, as well as the know-how to use them, is underscored by the total electrical blackout that we were actually experiencing aboard *Yvaledon*. Although we were not caught out after dark, as projected in the "what-if" scenario described above, that messy possibility was increasingly imminent as we closed in on Block. However, with that additional complication narrowly avoided, I shall return to relating events as they actually happened.

We had finally reached the channel breakwater (jetty), still under engine power alone, with only a mile to go across Great Salt Pond to our anchorage in front of the Narragansett Inn.

Having no dinghy for transportation ashore, we docked at the marina nearest the Narragansett Inn. The sun had set. We had just made it in before dark. Ashore we went to find a hot meal and a comfy room with a hot shower. One thing I particularly like about the Narragansett is that I can normally look out of any window on the harbor side of the building and see my boat at anchor. Although the accommodations are somewhat austere, the staff is very friendly and bend over backwards to be helpful. Since there would be no looking out at the boat at anchor this time, and with a hankering for somewhat more upscale accommodations, we decided to hoof it along the roadway for a mile and a half, or more, to the Spring House high on a hill.

The boat bags were on the heavy side, but the walking felt good. We arrived after dark while guests were casually walking the well-manicured grounds in relatively formal attire or enjoying libations and conversation in open chairs on the grounds or at tables under the extensive covered porches. All enjoyed the priceless views in every direction. We must have looked like low-wage help arriving late for work in some inner sanctum of the facility where guests would not ever have to be exposed to the likes of us. Shocked would they be to discover that we too were guests at the inn. For us to be allowed in as guests, either the Spring House was going rapidly down hill or we had to have just bought the place. Nevertheless, we were treated with the utmost courtesy and served a superb seafood dinner and wine on an outside porch. The rooms to which we were assigned were not quite what one would expect from the general ambiance of the inn's exterior and public areas, but they were comfortable and clean.

With only a day left to our long voyage, we were anxious to get started the next day. We replenished supplies of food, ice, and fuel. The wind blew all night. By midmorning, wind could be heard whistling here and there around the docks. The wind seemed to be coming out of the west-northwest. I decided to inquire of the dock master the actual wind speed and direction. His instruments were recording variable wind directions from west to northwest at speeds of between twenty-three and twenty-nine knots. I knew that we would be thrust into heavy seas as soon as we cleared the breakwater jetty. I also knew that the wind direction would be steady in the open water. I just did not know precisely from what direction it would be blowing.

A local boater, overhearing our conversation with the dock master, was incredulous that we were actually contemplating going out in that weather in our tiny boat. He watched as we began preparing the rig for departure. Unable to contain himself any longer, he exhorted, "You can't go out there in this weather in that boat!"

Surprised and a little startled by the sudden outburst, Lou and I stopped working and faced the source of such urgent and seemingly genuine concern.

He repeated his admonition, "You can not go out in this weather in that little boat!" The man was clearly upset.

I had not even considered not going out that morning. My only reason for inquiring about the wind was to help me decide whether I should take a reef in the main or not. In an attempt to allay the man's fears for our safety, I told him that we had been traveling for several weeks and had encountered conditions far worse than the weather that day and in more exposed waters than Block Island Sound. I told him that we were going to fly a storm jib and a reefed main. I pointed out some of the boat's safety features, such as sealed hatches, sturdy construction and full keel with a heavy lead weight for stability, and the EPIRB. As we donned our foul weather suits and inflatable life vests, he appeared to be a little more reassured but probably still thought we were crazy.

We cast off and backed out away from the dock, shifted into forward gear, and eased *Yvaledon* into the outbound channel.

As we left Great Salt Pond and motored along outer channel inside the protection of the breakwater, pulses began to race. We could see huge seas breaking beyond the jetty. Large waves crashed against the windward side of the breakwater and jettisoned high into the air. The aerial hydraulics glistened in the bright sunlight like a million liquid diamonds. As the wind tried to carry the spume over the jetty into the channel, the heavy spray and green water fell earthward like a heavy blanket onto the breakwater, draining through the labyrinthine cracks and crevices between the rocks and back into the sea. Only the foamy residue of white water trailed behind washing over the rocks, waiting to be smothered by the next dousing before the first had fully cleared.

Had I miscalculated? Were conditions worse than I anticipated? We could still turn back. That familiar knot in my stomach was back. Fear drew me toward retreat from the danger ahead tempting me to turn tail and withdraw to the safety of the harbor. The concerned boater's urgent words of warning shot back into my head like the voice of one's conscience before committing a grievous sin. But the adrenaline rush, well-earned confidence in the boat, and anticipation of another wild ride kept my hand steady on the tiller. Lou uttered not a sound. Neither of us spoke as we plunged headlong into that first deep trough.

The oncoming next wave lifted the bowsprit skyward. *Yvaledon* surged ahead, her powerful sails undeterred by the seas' coordinated attack on her hull. All that had been dry was wet with the sole exception of our spirits. This was the pure essence of adventure sailing. So few human beings ever come to know the thrill of life at the apex of existence. That was it, and we burned every moment into permanent memory to be savored at will endlessly into the future. That moment was stored alongside the many others we had collected along the way since leaving Noank weeks earlier.

On a very close reach, we were able to point directly at Watch Hill, the entry to Fishers Island Sound. But with a slight ebbing current, we would be drifted east of our target. We could have hardened our tack to windward and perhaps made Watch Hill on a single tack, but driving the boat that hard to windward would have incurred a wetter sail and required intense focus on the tiller, compass, and sail trim. That would have been way too much like work. Then, unless the wind changed, we would wind up motoring westward up the sound and home to Noank anyway. No matter. That was then, but now was now, and we were in sailor's heaven. The seas were running about five to seven feet high and were simple wind waves, not the vicious rip seas of Hog Island Channel or the far worse monsters of Pollock Rip. The waves were just large enough to permit *Yvaledon* to ride up and down over them without taking on much water at all. Smaller waves in the four-foot high range and more closely spaced would have been much wetter since the boat would slide down the back side of one wave and plunge into the base of the next, unable to level out in the trough and ease up the front side of the next wave as we were able to do in the larger seas.

Yachts began to pour out of Great Salt Pond heading northwest for Fishers Island Sound or more westerly into Long Island Sound. Those taking the more westerly route remained under power unless willing to spend the day beating to windward on long tacks against the current. All were large yachts that passed us by like we were standing still. We were soon alone again watching sterns and sails vanish over the horizon.

Seas diminished as the fetch decreased between us and the Connecticut and Rhode Island mainland. The afternoon also brought softer breezes and warmer temperatures. We soon shook the reef out of the main.

Upon reaching Watch Hill, the sails came down for the last time in preparation for the eight-mile ride against wind and current up Fishers Island Sound to Noank, Connecticut at the mouth of the Mystic River. After over three weeks, mostly at sea, we were headed home. Lou and I tucked everything in, Bristol fashion, for a yacht-like arrival at our home port. Motoring up Fishers Island Sound was a bitter-sweet ride—a little depressing that our long odyssey was over but at the same time exciting in that we were returning to a much easier life on land with all the conveniences of modern-day living and joyful reunions with family and friends.

As 7:00 p.m. approached, and the sun reddened and swelled in preparation for its mating ritual with the horizon, we gently approached the dock at Noank Shipyard. The air, soft and dry and still, the water calm and quiet, hardly a sound could be heard over the purr of our little engine. *Yvaledon* inched up to the dock, never touching it. We stepped out with lines in hand and tied her up bow and stern. In the melancholy silence of the evening, we began offloading our things from the cabin and sail lockers creating quite a pile of junk on the floating dock. Large, expensive yachts sat quietly in their slips on either side of us, the flicker of television screens bearing witness to the humanity within.

The setting sun was becoming a spectacular event, along with the full harvest moon rising in the night sky. We had to stop working and savor the moment. I had brought along a special sampling of eighteen-year-old Macallan single malt Scotch whiskey for just that occasion. Upon toasting everything imaginable, we sat in the cockpit and let the night silently fall around us. The gentle floating motion of the boat, the sky ablaze with stars, the full moon above a dark red horizon, the soft warm air, and the soothing influence of a fine Scotch whiskey. What a perfect setting! What a shame I had to waste it on Lou! He was probably thinking the same about me. Nevertheless, there's nothing wrong with sitting in the cockpit of a small boat in a quiet, beautiful harbor on the Mystic River, and marveling at the night sky with a dear friend and a bottle of fine whiskey.

CHAPTER XIV

BROACHED IN BLOCK ISLAND SOUND

I had planned on Sudden Death of the Twenty-First Century being the final chapter of this book. But during the development of the manuscript, I had an experience with my two oldest daughters that demanded an additional chapter. And I am quite sure that they will be most excited to become part of this thrilling adventure series, given they are still willing to refer to themselves as my daughters and have not disowned me.

So with a humbled and contrite heart, I dedicate this chapter to my wonderful and loving daughters and two very good sports, Donna and Valerie.

It all started out so innocently. A father and his two daughters set sail on a picture-perfect day for a glorious Labor Day weekend on Block Island, Rhode Island. Before a quartering breeze of five to ten knots, and with the sun coaxing clothing off the two girls down to their well-suited bikinis, *Yvaledon* glided silently along assisted by an ebbing current toward Wicopesset Passage at the eastern end of Fishers Island. The trip through that constricted passage is always fun as the current accelerates to several knots kicking up a rip sea that offers a short but exciting carnival-style ride. Running with the current, we were assured of a dry frolic. We all laughed and hooted our way through Wicopesset toward the open waters of Block Island Sound.

This was a day for the spinnaker and up it went. Setting the unstopped[5] sail directly from its turtle bag is always a challenge to get it up without hourglassing. Today was no exception. Donna "womaned" the tiller while I kept the sail from wrapping itself around the forestay in such a manner as to fill with air in two parts forming an hourglass-shaped embarrassment. After a defiant but brief attempt to impede proper deployment, the sail filled and snapped to attention yanking the boat forward at a brisk pace. The spinnaker promised to add interest and glamour to an otherwise long and humdrum journey to Block.

For several hours we sailed; Block looming ever larger and closer. About two-thirds of the way across Block Island Sound, a whale spouted a few points off the starboard bow. We all saw it. I had never seen a whale in such confined and sheltered waters before. The animal was headed in our general direction but not directly at us. We were transfixed. The improving detail, rendered by closing proximity, served only to increase my anxiety. The beast was oddly formed, not like any other whale I had ever seen. From a few hundred yards distant, the back appeared rough, not smooth. As the beast neared, I could see a large dorsal fin running the length of its back and deeply scalloped. What was this creature? It was big so it had to be a whale. Valerie blurted out, "What is that?" As the view gradually transitioned toward the beam, a space of several feet of clear, unbroken water could be seen from the forward part of its back to the knobby protrusion that spouted water and air. What kind of freak was this? At a distance of about fifty yards, it looked something like a real-life rendition of "Puff, The Magic Dragon." Again, Valerie said, "Is that a shark fin?" apparently referring to the scalloped dorsal. What we could see of the animal, from the aft end of its back to the knobby protrusion in the front, was every bit as long as our boat. The knobby protrusion raised out of the water revealing a conical-shaped head with two huge eyes and a beak (the knobby protrusion). I immediately realized that we might be looking at the largest leatherback turtle I had ever seen. I had seen two leatherback turtles on two separate occasions in Long Island Sound years before, both turtles only about six to eight feet in length. The largest leatherback ever recorded was about twelve-feet long. This animal was well over that. I began to notice other details characteristic of the leatherback, such as two secondary scalloped ridges on either side of the center dorsal ridge on an otherwise fairly smooth shell. The center ridge was about a foot or more in height above the shell. I never saw flippers or a tail. As the turtle passed, Donna yelled at me for her cell phone to take a picture—the one that I had just buried in my pocket for safekeeping. I struggled fruitlessly for the phone as the turtle sank out of sight, leaving us stunned and silent.

On we sailed to Block, all the while trying to digest what we had seen on the way. Approaching Great Salt Pond, the spinnaker had to come down, our attentions diverted by the demands of the busy harbor. Block Island is one of the few refuges that still have space to anchor. Most places are so choked with moorings that even a small craft like ours cannot be anchored safely. We motored over a mile to the far side of the harbor where we found a shallow anchorage in about four feet of water opposite the Narragansett Inn. This was perfect since we were staying at the Narragansett. Valerie guided the boat along the channel while I secured the sails. During our search for a spot to drop the hook, we drifted under idle power past one anchored boat after another waving and saying hello to the many people sitting in their cockpits enjoying an early evening libation and the late afternoon sun. As we passed one boat in particular, a man said, "Look out for the rock just ahead of you." No sooner did he say that than I saw the thing topping out less than a foot below the surface. I jammed the tiller hard to starboard just in the knick of time to avert a most embarrassing but probably harmless encounter. Since I was standing on the aft deck at the time, tiller in hand, like the commander of some great ship, I certainly would have been launched headfirst into my own cockpit in a rather undignified manner had we jolted to a halt upon that rock. I thanked the man profusely. In fact, I am still thanking him.

The plan was to spend the next day playing on the island and to return to Noank on the third day. After a gin and tonic and a wonderful meal on the veranda of the Narragansett overlooking the harbor and our boat, we showered and retired (passed out) in real beds for the night.

The next morning the girls were distressingly eager to get going. They wanted to rent bikes and tour the island. I was thinking, "I'm too old for this." But off we went. For at least six hours we peddled our asses off from one end of that hilly island to the other. In retrospect, I imagine that I was being prepunished for what I was about to inflict on them the following day. We stopped at the Southeast Lighthouse for water and to tour the magnificent structure. We then stopped at Mohegan Bluffs where, after gazing at the breathtaking vista, we climbed down 144 wooden steps—we all counted them and, amazingly, came up with the same number—to within about fifty vertical feet of the beach below. At the end of the stairs, one has to climb the rest of the way down over rocks to actually reach the stone littered beach. With so much raw material everywhere, people had erected stone cairns as far as the eye could see. Some were built on precarious promontories over a hundred feet above the beach. Of course, we had to build our own as well but at beach level. Finally, back up the rocks, up the stairs, and to the bikes on which we could rest while peddling to the next destination. Here, I must note one minor, but essential, detail. I carried Donna's treasure—her backpack full of rocks that she had collected on the beach—up the rocky path to the steps and up all 144 steps to our bikes. There, she generously reclaimed her backpack for the continuing bike tour. At long last, we returned the bikes and hit the bar at the Narragansett. Another incredible seafood dinner and then...and then...can you believe, those girls were ready for a night out! God help me! They mercifully left me behind.

Day three: The girls were up and ready to go as if they had slept the entire day before. After a hearty breakfast, we restocked on ice, rowed the dinghy back to the boat, and prepared to sail. The sky was gray, but the breeze was warm and inviting at least to me. Some guy in a motorboat near us said, "You're not going out in that boat today, are you?" That was not a question I wanted the girls to hear. Donna then said, "It's going to rain." Scoundrel that I am, as Valerie referred to me, I almost reflexively responded, "No, I checked the weather. There will just be a misting and a max of three-foot waves," meanwhile steaming at the busybody who spooked my crew. As I nudged *Yvaledon* gently forward with the engine, Donna pulled the anchor easily from the sandy bottom and cleaned it off by splashing it up and down in the water. She then hauled it up and secured it in its chocks on the deck. Responding to increasing power, *Yvaledon* churned a respectable wake toward the channel out into the open sound. As we proceeded across Great Salt Pond, sails were prepared for a downhill run. The spinnaker was readied for launch on the foredeck and the six-foot-long aluminum pole was rigged onto the mast. Working sails were set to begin our departure from Block. As we emerged from the channel past the breakwater into the open sound, dozens of large sailing yachts poured out of the harbor and blasted past us turning westward toward Long Island Sound. Our course was set for the more northerly target of Wicopesset Passage.

A little more detail than usual may be in order here to better understand the events about to unfold. The spinnaker pole serves as a specialized boom for the spinnaker sail. One end of the pole is attached to a ring on forward edge of the mast a few feet above the deck. The ring is part of a fitting that can be raised or lowered by sliding it up and down a track on the mast's leading edge.

The position of the ring is thus set to position the pole (which is kept horizontal) for the best sail shape to maximize boat speed. With the head of the sail fixed in position at the top of the mast, lowering the pole tends to flatten the sail while raising the pole allows the sail to assume a more cupped shape to better lift the bow and prevent driving the boat under in high winds. The pole is held in place with three lines: A "pole lift" extends from a turning block partway up the mast near the spreader and attaches to a bridle on the upper side of the pole to hold the pole horizontal and off the deck prior to setting the sail. Since the sail tries to lift the pole as it fills with air, a "downhaul" is attached to a bridle on the underside of the pole and secured to the deck to maintain the horizontal attitude of the pole after the spinnaker is set. The outboard end of the pole secures one corner of the spinnaker at one end of its lower edge, or foot, which in turn prevents the pole from swinging freely in a horizontal plane left and right. That corner of the sail is not attached to the pole directly, which is critically important for releasing the sail and spilling the wind but to a sheet which runs freely through a fitting at the end of the pole. The sheet then leads aft to a turning block at the stern and then forward to a winch in the cockpit. That sheet that passes through the end of the pole becomes the "guy" and is used to position the pole and sail with respect to the wind. All of this pole rigging was done as we prepared the sail for use.

The turtled sail (bag) was fastened to the deck at the bow, and the remaining sheet was attached to the other corner of the sail's foot. That sheet passed outside of everything (all the standing rigging) to a turning block at the stern on the side of the boat opposite the turning block for the guy then forward to a winch in the cockpit. These turning blocks on either side of the aft deck are where almost 90 percent of the driving force of the spinnaker sail is applied to the hull. The halyard was attached to the third corner at the head of the sail. The spinnaker is always stuffed into the turtle bag so that the three corners are peeking out of the top where lines can be readily attached to them. The spinnaker was ready to fly.

Now, just before hauling the sail out of the bag with its halyard, the pole was carefully positioned at right angles to the wind. In this case, the wind was coming from directly astern. The pole could, therefore, have been set on either side of the boat. I set the pole to port so that the boat would be inclined to yaw to port, rather than to starboard, in the following sea. A track slightly to port of the course line would be the safer choice since the rocks of and around Wicopesset Island lay off to starboard. Fishers Island lay safely off to port of Wicopesset Passage.

At the tiller, Valerie guided the boat as I hauled on the halyard freeing the sail from its turtle. The usual struggle to prevent a figure eight snafu kept me busy until the sail snapped to attention in perfect form. The little boat jumped like a rabbit nearly doubling her speed to about four knots. The sheet on the free corner of the sail was adjusted to maximize our speed. The breeze was a gentle five or six knots and the seas barely two feet in height—the perfect conditions for a spinnaker run to anywhere. The working jib, no longer helping, was lowered and secured to the bowsprit next to the now empty turtle.

The sun rose steadily higher in the overcast sky increasing its influence on wind and weather. Slowly and inexorably the wind increased. Ever so gradually, so went the seas. *Yvaledon* stepped up to about five knots but remained calm of demeanor.

The breeze continued to increase. Seas continued to build. *Yvaledon* became a little edgy as she began to sport a bone in her teeth and twitched occasionally at the tug of sheets from smart wind gusts. The girls sensed the change but were still at ease with the sail.

The freshening breeze began to lose its friendly caress. The huge spinnaker, pulling the boat along at near hull speed, began to threaten us with power and force. The first signs of instability demanded closer attention to tiller control. I noticed white caps here and there amongst the waves and began to think about how best to get the sail down. Should I stay at the tiller and put Valerie on the halyard so Donna and I could pull the sail into the cockpit? Valerie would not know how fast to feed the sail to Donna and might dump it into the water. Would Donna be better at the halyard? Maybe I should take the halyard and put Donna or Valerie at the tiller. But the tiller was becoming so sensitive that either of them might lose control of the boat causing a broach. Maybe I should handle both the tiller and the halyard myself. While agonizing over the "what-ifs," I concluded, hell, all I have to do is release the guy and spill the air from the spinnaker! Then the three of us can get the sail aboard easily. Besides, this spinnaker run was becoming really hot, not to be wasted.

Experience and age is often an advantage but is no guarantee of sound judgment. For those of you who have ever read a financial investment prospectus, do the words "Past performance is no guarantee of future results" come to mind? At that moment I had misjudged how totally consumed I would become, as the wind increased, in trying to evade imminent disaster under the evil press of a heartless sail. At the peril of losing all remaining confidence of my readers at this late time in the text, I am forced to admit that both girls were not wearing life jackets. This was not the highlight of my sailing life. God continued to punish me. But first, it might be helpful to further explore the influence of this mighty sail on the relatively diminutive boat.

Yvaledon has a tall, masthead rig; meaning, all jibs, including the spinnaker, fly from atop her thirty-foot mast. The spinnaker reaches down from the masthead over the sail's own broad shoulders to a wide foot near deck level that extends from one clew (corner of the sail) attached to the end of the six-foot pole on one side of the boat—the port side in this case—across the bow in a wide arc to the free clew on the opposite (starboard) side. Sail area is immense for the small size of the boat. Consequently, slight increases in wind speed and small gusts are magnified by the expansive sail area causing sharp, sudden accelerations and threats to overall boat stability.

Now, let's take a closer look at the stability issue for a moment. Picture in your mind this huge, parachute-like sail floating above and ahead of the boat dragging it through the water. Aside from being attached to the boat at each of the sail's three corners: one at the end of the pole, one at the top of the mast, and one free-floating at the end of a long line (the sheet); the sail is a free agent following the wind. Although the sail looks like it is pulling the boat through the water, it is actually *pushing* the boat through the water, and it is pushing the boat from the stern (at the turning blocks) much like one would push a pencil across the table by its eraser. As long as the pencil stays straight and aligned with its direction of motion, it keeps moving in a straight line. But as soon as the pencil gets even a little cocked to one side, continued pushing on the eraser quickly increases the cockeyed attitude of the pencil until it spins completely around and stops—similar to the action of a boat during a broach. The same kind of instability develops as a spinnaker "pushes" a boat faster and faster through the water. With the spinnaker "pushing" on the stern, each yaw of the boat in a following sea tends to misalign the boat with its direction of travel and increases the likelihood of a broach.

How is the sail "pushing" the boat? Anyone who's ever watched a boat sailing with a spinnaker can plainly see the sail pulling the boat along. That misperception is created by the position of the sail in front of the boat, which makes it look like the sail is pulling the boat. But if we review the way the sail is attached to the boat, the fact of pushing becomes most evident. Recall that the two sheets (the guy and free sheet) run from the sail at either end of the foot aft to turning blocks on each side of the boat at the aft most end of the deck then forward to cockpit winches. Almost all of the "pulling" force being applied by the sail is being exerted through the turning blocks on the stern. That is where the boat is being "pushed" through the water. A relatively small amount of force is being applied by the head of the sail to the top of the mast and there the boat is, in fact, being pulled along since the mast is forward of amidships.

So as each wind-driven wave catches up with the boat from behind and lifts the stern, it also carries the stern forward and slightly to the side as if to send the stern past the bow. As the wave continues on under the boat, it then lifts the bow allowing the stern to drop back into its original position behind the bow. This cycle, called yawing, is repeated AD infinitum as long as the wind blows. The stronger the wind and the higher the seas, the greater is the tendency of the boat to yaw in a following sea. Now, with the spinnaker pulling at the stern (pushing the boat) in a constant direction (like a finger pushing on the eraser end of a pencil), when the boat yaws to one side, the guy and sheet aggravate the yaw by assisting the wave in attempting to drag the stern past the bow. The person at the tiller, or helm, can minimize the yaw by turning the boat's rudder in a direction to counteract the yaw. If the timing of a yaw can be anticipated, the rudder can be artfully manipulated to prevent any yaw at all in modest conditions. In heavier weather, yawing can only be minimized.

Yvaledon was exceeding her design hull speed of over five knots. A large bow wave was cresting just below deck level on either side, and the boat was lurching incessantly in every direction. A deep hole (trough) amidships followed the bow wave. The water rose again to form a stern wave cresting near deck level giving the impression that the boat was trying to squat with the stern down and the bow up. Wind was up to ten to twelve knots, seas about four feet. *Yvaledon* was still responding well to rudder control although skittish as a frightened cat. The occasional collapse of the spinnaker's leading edge followed by the nerve-shocking snap of the sail back into full fill sent violent shudders throughout the entire hull and chills up and down my spine. Valerie expressed her opinion of the ride by puking over the side.

My focus was increasingly consumed with maintaining directional control of the boat. Seas had grown to five feet, wind to over fifteen knots. The girls had gone silent. I could sense a deepening fear about which I could do nothing. Valerie was seasick and had to lie down on the starboard seat. Seas were capping with foam, the wind hissed through the rigging. The boat was charging along at unprecedented speed. I could feel the hull trying to jump out of the water and plane, no longer trying to squat. I could not lose control of the boat or a horrendous broach would surely ensue, yet the tiller was so demanding I could not even reach across the cockpit to release the guy from the self-tailing winch without losing the boat. I dared not ask Donna to do it because of the possibility of her getting seriously hurt if she got her hand fouled in the line as it exploded from the winch to freedom. All I could do was ride the monster as long as possible.

Wind rose to over twenty knots, seas to six feet in height and continued building. The bow wave was cresting almost a foot above the deck on both sides. The stern was almost submerged. The spinnaker was slamming up and down as the boat plunged into a trough and rose with the next crest. I felt another surge in boat speed and watched incredulously as the bow wave began to move aft past the cabin, past the cockpit, and out of view astern. *Yvaledon's* bow hung in midair, her stern riding high, as she teetered on the crest of a breaking sea. The great sail aloft pulled her forward until she fell bow first over the crest and began charging down the front side of the wave! She then climbed up the back side of the next wave and through its crest as she began to advance through the sea faster than the waves themselves. Never in my life had I sailed in a displacement hull boat faster than the waves, but we were doing just that! The thrill of that ride was an adrenaline rush of the first order surpassed only by the fear of how it must end. For over half an hour we continued this frenetic pace through the seas leaving wave after wave behind as we all but surfed over the sea.

As each wave crest arrived amidships, I felt the greatest loss of rudder control, as if much of the rudder was briefly out of the water, which may have been the case. A particularly large sea coupled with the distraction of sighting another boat became my undoing. *Yvaledon* yawed ever so slightly more than usual to port but enough to exceed the ability of her rudder to control the yaw. The relentless tug of the sail at the stern hauled the boat around hard to port. The low, starboard rail bit into the sea stopping the boat dead in its tracks. *Yvaledon* rolled over onto her side, water pouring into the cockpit and over Valerie's reclined, screaming body. Six-foot seas broke over her hull, one after another crashing into the mainsail and helping the still full spinnaker hold and lock *Yvaledon* in a deadly, full broach. Donna climbed up onto the side of the cabin. She just stared down at me, frozen in fear by the obvious fear in my face. In my panic, I did not know how to unlock the broach. Should I cut the lines but which ones? Whatever I did had to be done fast or we would swamp. I regained enough composure to realize that all I had to do was release the guy, which I did. Like a shot, the guy disappeared from the port winch, through the aft turning block and then forward through the end of the pole. The boat instantly popped upright and sat quietly in the seaway as if nothing extraordinary had happened. The main luffed violently overhead. The spinnaker thrashed about, entirely forward of the hull, with deafening claps, restrained only by its halyard and a single sheet. The guy, still attached to the free corner of the flailing spinnaker, lashed the sea beyond the spinnaker like a great bullwhip sending small white geysers of spray into the air at every contact with the water. And we all sat in the cockpit awash up to our waists in seawater. Yet with all that noise and violence, there seemed to be a sense of calm and relief. Donna, however, again stared down at me, unable to move. I told her to get the bucket. Her face immediately relaxed, and she jumped up and disappeared below through the open companionway. As she explained later, with that command, she knew I was still in control and in charge and that we would be okay. I wish I had felt as confident in myself at that moment. After dumping the contents of the bucket, consisting of cleaning supplies, brushes, etc., onto the cabin floor below, she emerged with the empty bucket ready for action. She emptied the cockpit of as much water as possible with the bucket and then continued with a large sponge. I pulled in on the mainsheet to ease *Yvaledon* forward and reset our course for Wicopesset Passage.

I opened the starboard lifeline gate to facilitate retrieval of the sail, and the three of us pulled the spinnaker into the cockpit from under the main boom. After disconnecting both sheets, we stuffed the sail back into its bag. The first sheet was then coiled and secured in the cockpit. The second sheet could not be found even though both were there just minutes before. We must have stuffed it into the bag along with the sail. However, a thorough search of the bag turned up nothing. The missing sheet, which had served as the guy, had not been completely pulled back into the boat. With the boat moving nicely under the main alone in what had become eight-foot seas, the water had dragged the trailing guy slowly out of the cockpit and over the side while we tended to other things.

The sting of frustration at my own carelessness was quickly eclipsed by fear in Donna's face again. "Can I have a life jacket?" she begged as she began to cry. At the frightened sound of her trembling voice and the pleading look on her face, I had all I could do to keep from sobbing uncontrollably in empathy and guilt under the sudden, wrenching awareness of my negligence and irresponsibility for such abysmal safety discipline. I had violated a sacred trust of my own daughters to keep them safe. A glance around at the angry seas surrounding us pounded the stake of guilt yet deeper into my soul. We all donned life jackets for the rest of the ride home. Occasionally, even life's most important lessons have to be relearned. In this case, God spared me the cruelest punishment.

Once back on dry and stable land, and with shock wearing off, Valerie swore off sailing for the rest of her life. As far a she was concerned, she had had enough life threatening experiences as an army captain in Iraq to fill a lifetime. She did not need to expose herself to more of the same for recreation. Donna, on the other hand, was ready to go again.

That was in September of 2010. By November, Valerie had forgiven me most of my trespasses, and was accompanying me to see a live performance of *How to Succeed in Business without Really Trying* at the beautiful, restored, Victorian, Goodspeed Opera House in East Haddam, Connecticut. Following a most enchanting and entertaining matinee, we walked across the street to the Gelston House restaurant where we enjoyed a wonderful seafood dinner overlooking the beautiful Connecticut River. There, I plied my daughter with fine wine and gourmet food. We laughed and talked about everything and anything that came to mind. Conversation eventually came around to our fateful sail to Block Island a few months earlier. As we reminisced about all the fun we had on the island and on the sail over, Valerie volunteered that she might consider another sail to Block Island—"if the weather is good."

Fast forward to a sunny Sunday afternoon on the 24th day of July 2011. As soon as I finish this paragraph here in my study on the second floor of my charming Cape Cod style house in Glastonbury, Connecticut, I will make three copies of this chapter to take with us to Block Island on August 12. There, Donna, Valerie, and I will spend an afternoon on the porch of the Narragansett Inn sipping "adult beverages" and reviewing the text to "correct all of your (my) lies" and to ensure an accurate depiction of events as recalled by the three of us. I have been informed that the review will precede the sipping.

The preceding text is the "corrected" version.

"Yvaledon in a Full Broach"

APPENDIX A

Map of Magnetic North Migration

Appendix B

Personal Clothing and Loose Equipment List

Item:	Make:	Comments:
Clothing:		
Foul weather gear	Helly Hansen (Panorama jacket and Hybrid pants)	The jacket provided complete protection for 20+ hours of continuous spray and rain. The pants lasted only 4 hours before the membrane broke down and began to pass water like wet linen for both Lou and I. I have since replaced the Hybrid pants with HH Ocean Racing pants, which provide equivalent protection to the Panorama jacket.
Foul weather boots	Dubary (Fastnet boots)	The best boots I ever owned -- the only boots that did not chafe my calves and, unlike rubber boots, they breathe.
Boat shoes	Helly Hansen, and Sperry Billfish Topsiders	Both brands slip on wet, slick surfaces. Both need softer, grippier soles.
Baseball cap	Any	The cap keeps the foul weather jacket hood out of one's face, especially when looking up or from side to side, and provides additional protection from spray and rain.
Headlamps	Petzl, and Energizer	Both have white and red LED's and allow for hands-free operation, as opposed to a flashlight. However, headlamps are easily dislodged or brushed off one's head. A much better solution is a baseball cap with built-in white and red LED's.
Fast-dry shirts and pants	L.L.Bean	The shirts are tropic weight with SPF 40 sun protection factor, which was very effective. The clothing is comfortable and has great pockets.

Item:	Make:	Comments:
Fast dry underwear	Polartec, and Exofficio	The Polartec stitching, especially in the waist band, was scratchy and uncomfortable. The Exofficio was very comfortable. Both dried well.
Wool socks	L.L.Bean (Cresta Hiking Socks), and Smart Wool socks	Both are excellent. The wool was not itchy at all even when wet. Most amazing is that our feet never felt cold or even wet when totally soaked! The wet socks never "squished" while walking. The wool breathes well and was not "hot" on hot dry summer days.
Sailing gloves	West Marine (Amara)	Open tip gloves. I burned my finger tips on fast moving lines – recommend full-tip gloves. Gloves are most helpful in cool weather.
Ski goggles	Carrera	Non-fogging (double pane) for use during squalls, so crew can see into wind-driven rain and spray.
Sun hat	Any wide brimmed hat with under-chin tie	Helps keep cancer off nose, ears and lips.
Sun block	Neutrogena (SPF 55)	Not greasy. Recommended by my dermatologist. Very effective!
Mosquito repellant	Cutter (unscented)	Very effective!
Safety:		
Inflatable vest with strobe-light and whistle	Mustang (hydrostatic) vest, ACR (RapidFire) strobe, Storm (Safety) whistle	Auto-inflates only if submerged about 3 inches. Will not inflate from extended soaking by spray or rain. Very comfortable to wear. Has D-rings for safety tether. Every crew member wears one in foul weather, at night, and at all times offshore – not optional!

Item:	Make:	Comments:
Tether	West Marine	Attaches to inflatable vest D-rings.
PLB (Personal Locator Beacon) with GPS	ACR (ResQFix)	Registered with the NOAA Satellite and Information Service. Every crew member wears a registered PLB in foul weather, at night, and at all times offshore – not optional!
Seat cushions (throwable)	West Marine (PFD-IV)	To be thrown directly at anyone who goes overboard.
Flare kit	Orion (Signal Kit)	Contains hand-held flares, aerial flares with launcher, and signal mirror.
First aid kits	N/A	Homemade kit containing: Bactine liquid for minor burns, Polysporin antibiotic ointment for cuts, gauze pads, Band-Aids, cloth tape with dispenser, ibuprofen, and Uncle Bill's tweezers – best brand I ever used. This was our everyday kit.
	West Marine (500)	Serious injury / illness kit.
Radar reflector	Any	I don't know if any of them really work, but I use a small round one that I can hoist up the mast. I have since installed a Sea Me radar transponder that boosts the incoming signal from another boat before bouncing it back to the source. That makes my little boat look more like the Block Island ferry on anyone's radar screen – if someone's watching! I still carry the little round one in case I lose electrical power.
Cable cutters	Felco	To clear broken stays and shrouds.
Rigging knife with marlin spike	Myerchin (Crew)	To cut away fouled lines and loosen jammed knots.

Item:	Make:	Comments:
Bailing bucket	Any	Doubles as a potty – best to have two. They occasionally go overboard.
Communication:		
Wireless mike	Uniden (WHAM)	Allows the built-in VHF radio located in the cabin to be used remotely from the cockpit or on-deck.
Handheld VHF radio	ICOM (IC-M34)	Important back-up for the built-in VHF
Signal horn with spare canister	Falcon	Essential for safety in fog and at other times of reduced visibility. Also needed to signal passing intentions to approaching boats and to respond to horn signals from other boats.
Manual horn	Orion (Blaster)	Important back-up.
Cell phone	Verizon (Motorola submersible)	With 12-volt and 120-volt charger cords.
Navigation:		
Charts	NOAA (from OceanGrafix)	Full size paper charts covered every place we went. Important back-up for failed GPS or electrical system.
Chart covers	ULINE (2mil x 24" x 36")	Clear vinyl for full size NOAA paper charts folded in half. Waterproof and add heft to resist blowing overboard.
Navigation protractor	Sporty's (Super Plotter)	Made for aircraft -- ideal for boat cockpits and cramped spaces. Easier to use than marine equivalents.
Dividers	West Marine (Straight)	Preferred this to the "One-Hand" dividers
		.

Item:	Make:	Comments:
Pens, pencils, erasers and note pads	Any	Carried a generous assortment of all, including standard wooden and mechanical pencils, sharpener and spare leads.
Log book	Any	The more you use it, the easier to remember what you did, where and when, weather, etc. A voice recorder makes a good log book supplement.
Calculator	Radio Shack (Mity-Thin)	Solar powered.
Binoculars	Steiner (Commander Digital)	Outstanding product! The Fluxgate compass has no moving parts and provides accurate bearings in a seaway. Best binocular visibility I have ever experienced in low light and dark conditions. Auto-focus adds to ease of use.
Hand bearing compass	West Marine	"Hockey puck" – the only hand bearing compass that can be read while aiming – a major advantage for accurate readings. Stable and clear card markings. The dim internal light renders the compass useless at night. However, the Steiner binoculars (above) provide excellent bearings at night.
Beam lights	Golight (Profiler II)	A $300 light that does not work for very long in the rain! The light has no sealing against the weather that I could see and the plug for the charger cord rusted away. But while it worked, it was the best beam light I ever used with an almost laser-tight beam.
	Pro-Torx	A $20 light that never failed!

Item:	Make:	Comments:
Flashlights	Mag-Lite	Watertight, rugged and reliable! We used 3 sizes, all silver in color – more easily found in a dark cockpit or cabin.
	Smith & Wesson (Captain's)	White and red LED's. Excellent quality. AA-size light comes with useful belt holster. Black color not an issue when used with holster.
	Husky	The D-cell lights fell apart when dropped.
	Garrity	Good quality, but too dark in color – not easily located in the dark.
Charger cords	As required (12 V and 120 V)	For all devices that need them (120 V for shore based charging opportunities).
Repair / Maintenance:		
Tool kit	Any	I collected as many stainless steel and bronze tools as possible to minimize the impact on the compass. Add things as you need them.
Lube kit with all purpose oil, and	WD-40	Never be without a WD-40 spray can.
Teflon grease	Starbrite (PTEF)	Teflon grease is great for high temp applications, repels water and does not stain sail cloth or other fabrics -- way better than Lubriplate and other petroleum based grease for general purpose use.
Splicing and sail repair kit	Any	Be able to repair / replace lines and mend sails.
Spare batteries	As required	For all lights and electronics that need them.

Item:	Make:	Comments:
General cleaner	Fantastik (w orange)	Even removes some mildew. Other non-residue cleaners such as Windex, denatured alcohol, mineral spirits, etc. may also be useful.
Polish	Collinite's Fleetwax	Mildly abrasive – excellent results on metal, Fiberglass and plastics.
Brushes	Any	For cleaning.
Miscellaneous:		
Bottled water	Any	Used for drinking and cleaning. Aquafina comes in nice sturdy bottles.
Nutritional rebalance	Gatorade	Engineered to replace electrolytes lost by sweating, causing a loss of energy. Very effective.
Energy or meal replacement bars	Any	When you don't have time to eat anything else.
Fresh apples, celery sticks, raw carrot sticks, and dried fruit snacks	Any	Fresh apples, celery and carrots can last in ice or ice water for up to 3 weeks.
3 oz. cans of tuna salad and chicken salad	Any with peel-off tops	Tastier than plain canned tuna or chicken. Nutritious, easy to eat.
Coolers	Coleman (48 qt)	For extended travel. Does not have upper tray; an upper tray is very handy.
	Igloo (Playmate)	Does have upper tray – very effective.
Re-sealable plastic bags	Ziploc and Hefty	Re-sealable plastic bags will keep food dry even when sloshing around in ice water inside a cooler.

Item:	Make:	Comments:
Paper towels, toilet paper, face tissues	Any	Store spares in the re-sealable plastic bags.
Trash bucket and trash bags	Rubbermaid bucket	Closeable bags reduce odors.
Sponges	Any large size	For bailing and cleaning.
Boat bags	L.L.Bean	Zip-top bags help protect from rain and keep things contained if knocked over. Incredibly, L.L.Bean does not waterproof their "boat" bags, so you can't even put them down on a wet surface safely. I used 303 Products (Fabric Guard) inside and out to waterproof the bags. That works.
	Best American Duffle	BAD bags are excellent and really waterproof.
Sleeping bag with liner and pillow	L.L.Bean (Adventure bag, Coolmax liner, Stowaway down pillow)	The Adventure bag is slightly tapered – perfect for a V-berth, but not extremely tapered like a "mummy" bag. The CoolMax liner was very comfortable in hot weather. I sometimes used it on top of the bag. The down pillow was very comfortable.

Note:
We always carried the following items back and forth between the boat and shore when traveling in the dingy:

- Flashlight for use at night if returning to the boat after dark.
- Signal horn for use in the fog to avoid being hit by approaching boats.
- Hand bearing compass to find the boat when returning to it in the fog or at night.
- Foul weather jacket in case it starts to rain or we take on spray in a head wind.
- Cell phone and hand-held VHF.
- Floating cushions (PFD-IV) for safety and comfort.

APPENDIX C

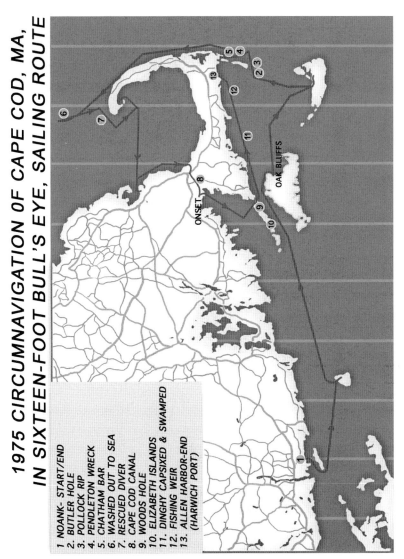

1975 Circumnavigation of Cape Cod, Massachusetts,
in a Sixteen-Foot Bull's Eye -- Sailing Route

APPENDIX D

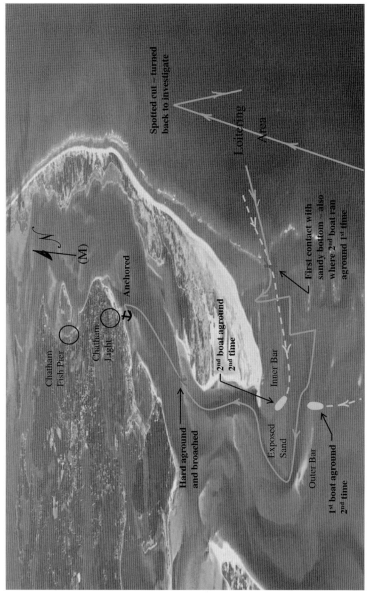

Aerial Photo of Chatham Bar, Circa
1977, with 1975 Sailing Track

APPENDIX E

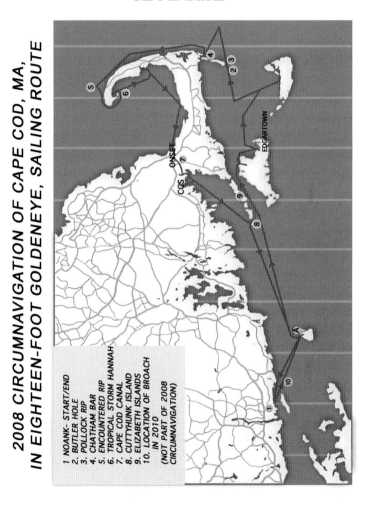

2008 Circumnavigation of Cape Cod, Massachusetts, in
Yvaledon, an Eighteen-Foot Goldeneye -- Sailing Route

APPENDIX F

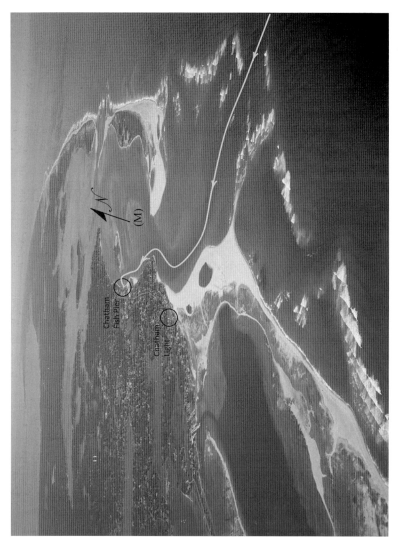

Aerial Photo of Chatham Bar, Circa
2009, with 2008 Sailing Track

GLOSSARY OF TERMS

Abaft – Toward the stern relative to some object – aft of.

Abeam – At right angles to the centerline of a boat in a horizontal plane – half way between fore and aft.

Aft – At or near the stern (rear) of a boat; also used meaning "aft ward" (opposite of forward) or toward the stern of a boat (same as astern).

Aft spring – A line used to prevent a boat or ship from moving aft along a dock and runs generally parallel to the length of the craft.

Against the wind – Sailing with the wind blowing from any direction forward of abeam.

Aground – Onto or on the ground, especially the shore, a reef, a rock, or in shallow water.

Amidship – In or toward the middle of a boat or ship. Also, along the centerline of a boat or ship.

Anchor – A hook-like device designed to prevent or slow the drift of a boat or ship by gripping the sea floor and attached to the vessel by a line and/or chain.

Anchor chain – A length of chain connecting the anchor to the anchor rode or to the vessel directly.

Anchor mooring – See **Mooring**.

Anchor rode (or rode) – The line connecting a short anchor chain to the vessel or the chain itself if no line is used. The chain and line combination is used primarily on smaller boats. The short length of chain prevents chafing of a soft line on rocks and other sea floor debris.

Arc – A segment of a circle.

Astern – At or toward the stern (rear) of a boat.

Atoll – A ring-shaped coral island and reef enclosing a lagoon and surrounded by open sea.

Awash – Covered with water.

Azimuth – Same as a bearing for use in dead reckoning. An azimuth is the direction of an elevated or celestial object (such as a star) in a spherical coordinate system projected onto a reference plane such as chart.

Back azimuth – The bearing or azimuth to an object away from which one is travelling.

Ballast – The weight at the bottom of and inside a boat's or ship's hull above the keel, or at the bottom of an extended keel, such as in a sailboat, to provide stability to resist heeling.

Bar – Same as a sand bar.

Beam – The maximum width of a boat or ship.

Beam ends – The end points of an imaginary line across a boat or ship at its widest location. For example, sailing extremely heeled as, "on her beam ends."

Beam reach – Sailing with the wind blowing from abeam.

Bearing – Direction of an object expressed as a compass reading, a direction as shown on a chart, or a direction relative to the heading of a boat.

Beat to windward (or beat) – Same as close hauled in moderate to heavy weather.

Before the wind – Same as with the wind.

Bell buoy – A buoy with a single tone bell.

Bend on – To install a sail on a boat, ready to deploy.

Bilge – The area inside the bottom of a boat below the lowest flooring.

Block – A pulley used on a boat to gain mechanical advantage or to change the direction of a line under tension.

Boat bag – An open canvass bag for carrying personal belongings aboard a boat.

Bobstay – A stay used to support the bowsprit from the underside, usually attached, or anchored, to the stem.

Bone it its teeth – The raised, frothy portion of a bow wave caused by a fast moving vessel, which from a distance suggests a bone in the mouth of an animal.

Boom – The horizontal spar that supports the foot of a sail.

Bow – The front part of a boat or ship.

Bow cheeks – The forward most sides of the hull on either side of the stem.

Bow line – A line used to secure the bow of a boat or ship to a dock.

Bowsprit – A spar that juts forward from the bow of a sailing vessel to which mast stays and sail stays are attached.

Bow wave – A continuous wave formed by the bow of a vessel moving through the water, which radiates outward from the vessel in a V-shaped pattern.

Breakwater – A barrier (usually man-made) that protects a harbor or other coastal area from the full force of the sea.

Broach – To lose control and twist sideways to the wind and sea in heavy weather such that the boat or ship rolls over onto its side in danger of capsizing, swamping, or sinking.

Broad reach – Sailing with the wind blowing from any angle between abeam and directly astern.

Broadside – The side of a boat or ship above the waterline.

Buoy – A large anchored float, often equipped with a light, bell, gong, whistle, and/or radar reflector, which serves as a guide or warning to boats and ships.

Also, a float marking the location of an anchor mooring, or a small float marking the location of a lobster, crab or other fish trap (pot).

Bulkhead – A vertical, or nearly vertical, partition in a boat.

Canoe stern – A stern that is pointed, like a bow, rather than squared off to form a transom.

Catboat – A sailboat with a wide beam and a single fore-and-aft sail on a mast located at, or very close to, the bow of the boat.

Centerboard – A retractable keel that pivots out of a slot in the hull of a sailboat. The slot is framed by a narrow, box-like structure (**Trunk**) that rises well above the waterline to keep water out of the boat.

Center-of-effort – The central point on a sail where, if a force were applied in the same direction as the wind, would have the same effect on the boat as the wind blowing on the entire area of the sail.

Center-of-lateral plane – The central point on the underbody of the hull where, if a force were applied perpendicular to the boat's centerline, would have the same effect on the boat as the water pressing evenly against the underbody to resist sideways motion, or leeway.

Chain plate – A sturdy, metal strap used to anchor a shroud or stay to the hull of a boat or ship.

Channel – A sea floor trench of deep, usually navigable, water, especially one that has been deepened by dredging.

Chart – A map with detailed information for use in navigation.

Chock – A device on the deck of a boat or ship, usually at its rail, to guide a line used to secure the vessel.
Also, any device used to secure another object. Anchor chocks secure an anchor to the deck of a boat or ship.

Chop – Steep, rough waves.

Cleat – A device with two projections pointing in opposite directions to which a line can be tied to secure a boat or a sail.

Clew – The aft, lower corner of a fore-and-aft sail. Both lower corners of a spinnaker are referred to as clews.

Clew outhaul – A short length of line used to pull the clew toward the aft end of the boom to tighten the foot.

Close hauled – Sailing as close to windward as possible without losing speed due to a partially collapsing sail.

Close reach – Sailing with the wind blowing from any angle between close hauled and abeam.

Close to the wind – Sailing close to the direction the wind is coming from.

Club (or club boom) – A short, curved boom attached only to the tack of a sail at one end and to the clew at the aft end, and holds the sail in the proper shape for sailing hard to windward. This allows a jib to be self-tacking.

Cockpit – The on-deck sitting area of a boat and from where the boat is usually steered.

Comber – A long, high, breaking wave that crashes onto a beach.

Comber field – An area of combers.

Coaming – The raised edging around a cockpit or hatchway on a boat or ship to keep out water.

Companionway – An opening in a bulkhead for access to the interior of a boat or ship and often combined with a hatchway.

Compass – A direction finding device usually with a free-swinging, magnetized needle that consistently points to magnetic north.

Compass card – A circular card with points of the compass marked in numbers or letters and attached to the magnetized needle.

Compass deviation (or deviation) – magnetic compass error induced by nearby steel or other magnetic objects – anchors, tools, radios, sound system speakers, electric power lines, etc. Deviation is expressed in degrees and minutes either above (+) or below (-) the correct magnetic compass reading.

Cordage – Ropes and cords collectively, especially the lines and rigging of a boat or ship.

Course – The planned direction or route of travel.

Course line – Any line representing a course. A line of position plotted on a chart, parallel or substantially parallel to the intended course of a craft and showing whether the craft is to the right or left of its course.

Crest – The top of a wave.

Cuddy cabin (or cuddy) – A small cabin in a boat, not tall enough to stand in.

Current – Same as tidal current.
Also, a river current.

Current velocity – The speed and direction of a current.

Cut – A trench, usually dredged, through a sand bar for boat navigation.

Also, a canal. See **Land cut**.

Dead reckoning – The navigational technique of determining position from a previously known or determined position using basic navigational instruments including a chart, compass, timepiece, speed measuring or estimating, binoculars, protractor, dividers, etc.

Dead run – Same as downwind.

Deck – The level walking surface of a boat that runs from side to side and from front to back.

Deck fill-pipe – A tightly covered opening in the deck of a boat or ship through which fuel or water tanks can be filled.

Deck pipe – A small, covered opening in the deck of a boat or ship for access to the interior for chain, lines, fluids or utilities.

Degree – 1/360th of a full circle.

Deviation – Same as compass deviation.

Dinghy – A small boat that is towed behind or carried on a larger boat.

Dividers – A navigational instrument consisting of two hinged legs with pointed ends that can be separated to a desired spread to transfer or measure distances on a chart.

Dock – A structure running along the shore or jutting out into the water for permanently mooring or temporarily berthing boats and/or ships.

Also, the process of approaching and landing against such a structure.

Dodger – A sheltering, frame-supported, canvas screen on a boat to protect from wind and spray, often equipped with non-glass (vinyl) windows.

Dogged down – Pulled down tight using a cam-action closure or threaded device.

Double reef – The reduction of about one half to two thirds of a sail's total area using the second (up from the boom) set of reef points on the sail.

Downhill run – Same as downwind.

Downhaul – A line attached to the head of a sail to pull the sail down and hold it down – used most often on a jib.
Also, a line used to pull the forward end of a boom down to tighten the luff of the sail.
Also, same as spinnaker pole downhaul.

Downwind – Sailing directly with the wind, in the same direction that the wind is blowing – wind from directly astern.

Douse – To lower or remove a sail.

Draft – The vertical distance from the waterline of a boat or ship to the lowest part of its hull, which is the minimum depth of water required to float the vessel.

Draw – To need a particular depth of water to float a boat or ship.

Drift – To be carried along by a current of water or air, usually without purpose or direction.

Due – Directly and exactly, as in due north.

Ease – To let out or slacken line that is too tight or a sheet to change the angle of the sail relative to the wind.
Also, to bring the helm, tiller, or rudder of a vessel slowly amidships.

Ebb current (or ebb) – The flow of an emptying body of water as a result of a falling tide.

EPIRB – An Emergency Position Indicating Radio Beacon that sends out a radio signal in the event of an emergency for rescue crews to respond to and locate and is carried on or attached to the outside of a vessel.

Fair current – A current that carries a vessel in the general direction of intended travel.

Fender – A soft, protective device hung over the side of a vessel to prevent damage from rubbing against a dock or another boat or ship.

Fetch – The distance a wind has available to increase wave height.

Flood current (or flood) – The flow of a filling body of water as a result of a rising tide.

Fluke – Either of the wide blades of an anchor.

Following sea – A sea coming from astern.

Foot – The lower edge of a sail.

Foot rope – A rope sewn into the foot of a sail for strength.

Fore – At or near the bow (front) of a boat.

Fore-and-aft rig – A sailing rig with sails set mainly along the line of the keel rather than perpendicular to it.

Foredeck – The forward part of a boat's deck.

Forward – Toward the bow (front) of a boat.

Forward spring – A line used to prevent a boat or ship from moving forward along a dock and runs generally parallel to the length of the craft.

Foul current – A current that impedes the travel of a vessel along its intended route.

Fresnel lens – A ribbed glass lens surrounding a bright light, designed to project the light along a flat plane parallel to the ocean surface and is typically used in light houses, lighted buoys, and older running lights.

Furl – To roll up or gather in and secure a sail on a spar or a stay.

Gaff-rigged – A mast or sailing vessel rigged with one or more four sided, fore-and-aft sails with the upper edge supported by a spar (gaff) extending aft from the mast.

Genoa (or genoa jib) – A large, light air jib that overlaps the mast and is often referred to as a jenny.

Gimbal – A device consisting of two rings mounted on axes at right angles to each other so that an object supported on these rings, such as a compass card, will remain suspended in a horizontal plane regardless of the motion of the compass housing (or the boat or ship).

Gong buoy – A buoy with a set of three or four gongs each having a different tone.

Gooseneck – A heavy fitting that connects the boom to the mast and anchors the tack of the sail.

Green water – Water with little or no bubbles and froth, sometimes referred to as "solid water."

Ground track – Same as track.

Gunwale – The upper edge of the side of a vessel.

Guy – The spinnaker sheet employed to position the spinnaker pole.

Halyard – A line used to raise and lower a sail or flag.

Hand-bearing compass – A portable, compact, hand-held compass to measure a bearing or azimuth to a given target and to determine user location.

Hard on the wind – Same as close hauled.

Hard to windward – Same as close hauled.

Hatch (or hatchway) – An opening in a horizontal surface, such as a deck or cabin top, for personnel access, loading and unloading, ventilation and light.

Head – A boat's or ship's toilet.
Also, the top corner, or uppermost area, of a sail.
Also, to be forced away from the course or course line by a change in wind direction.

Heading – The direction in which a boat is pointed (but not necessarily travelling) as given by a compass reading.

Headwind – A wind blowing from directly ahead, against a vessel's heading – applies to a vessel under mechanical or human power.

Heave to – To set the sails so that a boat or ship sits motionless, or nearly so, while heading into the wind in a seaway except for drifting.

Heavy seas – Large, rough waves.

Heavy weather – High winds and rough seas or stormy conditions.

Heel – To lean over to one side.

Helm – A spoked wheel for steering a boat or ship.

Helmsman – One who steers using a helm.

Hobbyhorse – To pitch in a seaway.

Hull – The main body of a boat, excluding the deck and other attached parts.

Into the wind – Same as against the wind.

Jack line – A line used to restrict or control the freedom of a sail, a spar, or a person. For example, sail slides can be attached to a jack line instead of directly to the lower portion of the sail luff to allow the sail to fold down onto the boom for reefing or furling.

Also, a jack line may be strung from bow to stern along a deck for crew members to attach safety harness tethers to while moving about the deck.

Jenny – Same as Genoa.

Jetty – A man-made breakwater that juts out from the land.

Jib – A small triangular sail forward of the mast or masts.

Jibe – To make a fore-and-aft sail swing across a boat from one side to the other when sailing downwind (wind blowing from behind).

Jiffy reefing – A reefing system utilizing a combination of lines, hooks and grommets that can be used to pull the sail down quickly to a set of reef points which, in turn, can be used to secure the sail to the boom.

Keel – The main structural element of a boat or ship extending along the centerline of its bottom from bow to stern and sometimes downward into the water for extra stability.

Ketch – A sailboat with two masts, both rigged fore-and-aft: a mainmast and a shorter mizzenmast abaft the mainmast but forward of the rudder post.

Key – A small, low island of fossilized coral (or coral and sand) found in tropical ocean waters.

Knockdown – A sudden and severe increase in the angle of heel of a sailboat due to a sharp wind gust.

Knot – A unit of speed equal to one nautical mile per hour, or about 1.15 mph.

Also, the result of a line interlaced with itself or with another line and pulled tight.

Land cut – That portion of a canal that is cut through the land. The total length of a canal can include a dredged channel beyond the land cut.

Latitude – An imaginary, circular line (called a parallel) around the Earth's surface that is parallel to the equator, and is measured in degrees and minutes either north or south of the equator.

Lazarette – A storage space below deck near the stern of a boat or ship.

League – An imprecise measure of distance equal to approximately three nautical miles.

Lee – The sheltered side or area away from the wind.
Also, same as leeward.

Leech (or leach) – The edge of a sail farthest from its supporting mast or stay (usually the aft edge).

Lee helm – The need to push the tiller to leeward or turn the helm to prevent a boat or ship from turning away from the wind.

Leeward – Situated away from the wind in a lee.

Leeway – Motion or drift sideways away from the course line.

Lifeline – A safety line that runs around the perimeter of a vessel's deck and is supported by vertical stanchions.

Lift – A change in wind direction permitting a change of heading closer to the course or course line.
Also, the effect of a current that drifts a vessel closer to the course or course line.

Line – A rope or wire cable that has been fashioned into a useful length of cordage for a specific purpose usually associated with a boat's rigging, handling, docking, or mooring.

Longitude – An imaginary, circular line (called a meridian) around the Earth's surface that passes through both the north and south poles and is measured in degrees and minutes either east or west from the prime meridian that passes through Greenwich, England.

Lubber line – A fixed line or pin attached to the forward end of the compass housing close to the compass card to indicate a vessel's heading.

Luff – To allow a sail to flap as a result of sailing too close to the wind.

Also, the edge of a sail closest to its supporting mast or stay (usually the forward edge).

Luff rope – A rope sewn into the luff of a sail for strength.

Magnetic north (North Magnetic Pole) – The point on the surface of Earth's Northern Hemisphere where a compass needle points vertically downward – near but not at true north. See Appendix A for more detail.

Main – Same as mainsail, and can also be used to refer to the mainmast on a boat with more than one mast.

Main hatch – The primary access into a boat or ship.

Mainmast – The tallest or only mast on a boat and supports the mainsail.

Mainsail – The largest and most important sail on a boat or ship.

Mainsheet – The line that controls the angular position of the mainsail on a sailboat or sailing ship.

Mast – A vertical spar that supports one or more sails on a boat or ship.

Masthead – The top of a mast.

Masthead rig – A sailboat rig designed to allow all jibs, including the spinnaker, to fly from the top of the mast with jib stays and halyards supported at the masthead.

Meridian – An imaginary, circular line of longitude.

Minute – One sixtieth of a degree of arc; the distance along the earth's surface at the equator that corresponds to one minute of arc is defined as one nautical mile.

Mizzenmast (or mizzen) – A mast aft of the mainmast and shorter than the mainmast on a two-masted sailing vessel; also the aftmost mast on a three masted ship.

Mooring (anchor mooring) – A semi-permanent structure that includes a heavy anchor on the sea floor with a length of chain and/or line supported by a small, floating buoy to mark its location and used to secure a boat or ship away from shore for extended periods of time.

Moorings of other types can be shore based and supported by structures such as docks, wharfs, piers, or jetties.

Also, the process of attaching a boat to a mooring.

Mooring buoy – The floating buoy used to mark the location of an anchor mooring.

Mooring pennant – A short length of line permanently attached to a mooring buoy and used to attach a boat to the mooring.

Motor-sail – To sail with the engine running in forward gear.

Nautical Mile – The distance of one minute of arc of longitude at the equator or one minute of arc of latitude along any meridian, about 1.15 statute miles.

Off the wind – In a direction away from where the wind is coming from.

On the wind – In a direction toward where the wind is coming from.

Overcanvassed – Too much sail for the prevailing wind conditions.

Overhang – That portion of a hull above the waterline that extends forward or aft of the waterline.

Painter – A line used to tow a dinghy behind another boat or to secure it to a mooring.

Parallel – An imaginary, circular line of latitude.

Pier – A large dock for commercial, industrial, and/or military boats and ships, and may support additional smaller docks, a roadway, parking, buildings and other structures and facilities.

Piloting – The navigational technique of determining position by comparing objects that can be seen such as buoys, lighthouses, rocks, cliffs, water color (depth), islands and other land outcroppings, etc.; things that can be measured, or felt, such as water depth and submerged objects by sounding; and others that can be heard such as bells, gongs, whistles, horns, etc. with symbols on a chart.

Pitch – To rotate about a horizontal axis such that the bow and stern of a boat or ship move up and down in a seesaw motion.

PLB – A Personal Locator Beacon that sends out a radio signal in the event of an emergency for rescue crews to respond to and locate and is worn or carried on the person.

Point – One of the 32 direction markings on a compass that is not marked in degrees.

Also, the distance between any two adjacent compass markings equal to 11 degrees 15 minutes.

Pole lift – Same as spinnaker pole lift.

Port – The left side of a boat or ship when facing forward.

Also, an opening in the hull or cabin for access, light, or viewing.

Also, a place by the sea or waterway where boats or ships can dock.

Port beam – The extreme left center of a vessel.

Port bow – The left front part (quadrant) of a boat or ship.

Port tack – Sailing with the wind blowing from the port side of the boat or ship, sails set on the starboard side.

Port quarter – The left rear part (quadrant) of a boat or ship.

Pot – Trap for catching lobsters, crabs or other fish on the sea floor.

Protractor – A navigational instrument for measuring angles, marked with degrees of a circle, and used to measure bearings on a chart.

Pulpit – A sturdy structure at the bow or stern of a vessel to provide safe containment of personnel on a deck. Lifelines often connect bow and stern pulpits.

Quartering – Wind or sea coming from a vessel's port or starboard quarter.

Radar reflector – A device, similar to a mirror, that bounces a radar signal from a nearby vessel back to that vessel to indicate the presence, direction, and approximate range of the vessel with the reflector.

Radar transponder – An electronic device that receives a radar signal from a nearby vessel and boosts it to a higher energy level before transmitting it back to the sending vessel. This provides the sending vessel with a stronger image on its radar screen than a simple, reflected signal can provide.

Rag-bagger – A sailboat or the sailor of a sailboat (slang).

Rail – The outer edge of a boat's deck.

Range – The distance between two things.

Also, the distance or area of effective operation.

Reach – Sailing with the wind blowing from any angle between close hauled and downwind.

Reciprocal heading – A heading 180 degrees away from the given heading.

Reduce sail – To take sail in by reefing, furling or removing sail to leave less sail area exposed to the wind.

Reef – A section of sail that has been gathered in and tied down to reduce the sail's effective area (See **Single reef** and **Double reef**).

Also, the process of reducing sail area, as in reefing the main, meaning to take, or put, a reef in the mainsail.

Also, a ridge of earth below the water's surface creating an area of water significantly shallower than the surrounding water, and which may be exposed during falling tides.

Reef points – A set of points on a sail, each containing a small line, or tie, extending on either side of the sail, and arranged in a straight line parallel to the boom and far enough above the boom so that the sail can be lowered until the ties can be wrapped around the boom to secure the reef.

Rig – To fit out a boat or its masts with sails and rigging.

Also, the arrangement of sails and masts on a boat or ship, such as a sloop rig.

Rigging – The ropes, wires, cables, chains and other hardware that support the masts and control the sails of a boat or ship.

Righting moment – The torque exerted by moving a sailing vessel's ballast off center to counteract the force of the wind causing the boat or ship to heel and is typically expressed in foot-pounds or newton-meters. Ten foot-pounds is the torque exerted by a ten pound weight at the end of a one foot long moment arm, or a five pound weight at the end of a two foot arm, etc.

Rip – An area of rough water characterized by steep, sharp waves formed by a current of water running in the opposite direction of, or against, the wind.

Rode – Same as anchor rode.

Rogue wave – An abnormally large, unpredictable wave that forms on a seemingly random basis in the oceans.

Roll – To rotate about a horizontal axis parallel to the vessel's centerline.

Roller reefing / furling – A system for either reefing of completely furling a sail by winding it around a rotating stay. This can be done for a jib or for a mast-supported sail by locating the rotating stay within the mast.

Roller-reefing – A reefing system whereby a sail can be rolled around the boom in window shade fashion to reduce its exposed, or effective, area. Sails are not furled in this manner.

Rudder – A steering device for a boat or ship, usually in the form of a pivoted blade below the waterline, mounted at or near the stern and controlled by a wheel or tiller (handle). Rudders are often mounted (hinged) to the aft edge of the keel for protection from damage.

Rudder post – A long pole attached to the forward edge of a rudder, which extends upward through the deck where it is attached to a wheel or tiller (handle) by which the rudder is controlled.

Running before the wind (or running) – Sailing within 20 degrees of downwind (a dead run).

Running lights – Nighttime navigation lights to identify the position and orientation of a boat or ship. Basic running lights include a red port light, green starboard light, and white stern light. A white bow light identifies a boat or ship under mechanical power.

Running rigging – Rigging used for raising, lowering and controlling sails.

Sail locker – An opening, usually in a boat's cockpit, for storing sails and related lines and gear.

Sail plan – The side elevation of a sailing vessel showing all sails and spars and some or all of the standing rigging, as if set directly fore-and-aft so that the true proportions are visible.

Sail slides – Small fittings attached to the luff of a sail to engage a slot or track on the aft edge of the mast and attached to the foot of the sail to engage a similar slot or track on the upper edge of the boom.

Sail stops – Short lines used to secure a furled or lowered sail or to tie down a sail to a deck or railing.

Sand bar (or bar) – A shallow, underwater reef made primarily of sand (or loose, ground-up coral).

Scope – The length of an anchor or mooring line in use.
Also, the ratio of length of an anchor or mooring line in use to water depth.

Screw – The propeller of a boat or ship.

Scud – To sail with a strong wind blowing from astern.

Sea – The disturbance and motion of the ocean surface, or the waves themselves.

Also, a single wave.

Seaway – An ocean surface where conditions are moderate to rough.

Sea-kindly – Sails easily in a rough sea with little or no pounding, shuddering, or other distressing motion.

Seaworthy – Suitable or in a fit state to sail safely on the ocean.

Second reef – Same as a double reef.

Self-tacking – A sail that can reset itself on the opposite tack without crew assist.

Self-tailing – A winch that needs no pulling force on the tail end of the sheet, halyard, or other line coming off the winch drum. A non-self-tailing winch requires an extra hand (or hands) to keep the tail end of the line tight enough to prevent its slipping on the drum.

Sextant – A navigational instrument used to measure the angle from the horizon to a celestial body such as the sun, moon or a star and, along with the time the measurement is taken, can be used to determine position on a nautical chart.

Shank – The main shaft, or stem, of an anchor.

Shallows – Water that is not deep and presents the possibility of a boat running aground – may be an area of one or more shoals.

Sheet – A line that controls the angular position of a sail on a sailboat. The sheet is not the sail!

Shoal – An area of shallow water where a boat can run aground.

Shorten scope – To pull in anchor line to reduce the horizontal distance from the boat to its anchor.

Short rig – A sailboat or ship with a short mast or masts compared to the length of the hull. This is a subjective judgment compared to the average proportions of similar sailing vessels and has no mathematical definition.

Shroud – A line used to support a mast from the side of a sailing vessel.

Single hand – To sail alone as a crew of one.

Single reef – The reduction of about one quarter to one third of a sail's total area using the first (lowest) set of reef points on the sail.

Slip – A small, floating dock designed for a single boat or for two boats, one on each side.
Also, the space between two docks, piers, or pilings for a boat or ship to dock.

Sloop – A sailboat with a single mast and a fore-and-aft rig with one sail aft of the mast and one sail forward of the mast.

Solid water – Same as green water.

Sounding – determining water depth by electronic measurement or by dropping a weighted line over the side until it hits bottom and measuring the resulting length of line.
Also, the resulting reading of water depth.

Spar – A sturdy pole that supports one or more sails on a boat.

Spinnaker – A large, triangular, parachute-like sail set at the front of a sailboat for running before the wind.

Spinnaker pole – A spar used to position and control a spinnaker.

Spinnaker pole downhaul (downhaul) – The line used to hold a spinnaker pole down in the horizontal position while the spinnaker is deployed.

Spinnaker pole lift (pole lift) – The line used to support a spinnaker pole from above to keep it horizontal prior to spinnaker deployment.

Spinnaker stops – Small, easily broken strands of cordage used to furl a spinnaker ready for deployment.

Spreader – A short strut part way up a mast to hold a shroud out and away from the mast for improved support of the mast – always used in pairs on either side of the mast.

Spring line (or spring) – A line used to prevent a boat or ship from moving forward or aft along a dock and runs generally parallel to the length of the craft.

Spume – foam resulting from a mixture of water and air.

Stanchion – A vertical post mounted along the edge of a vessel's deck to support a lifeline.

Standing rigging – Rigging permanently positioned to support masts and other spars and some sails.

Starboard – The right side of a boat or ship when facing forward.

Starboard beam – The extreme right center of a vessel.

Starboard bow – The right front part (quadrant) of a boat or ship.

Starboard quarter – The right rear part (quadrant) of a boat or ship.

Starboard tack – Sailing with the wind blowing from the starboard side of the boat or ship, sails set on the port side.

Stay – A line used to support a mast or other spar in the fore-and-aft direction.
Also, a line used to support a fore-and-aft sail that is not attached directly to a mast.

Stem – The extension of the keel at the forward end of a boat or ship, which rises from the keel to the main deck.

Step – To install a mast in a boat or ship.
Also, the fitting or depression into which the base of the mast is inserted and secured.

Stern – The rear part of a boat or ship.

Stern line – A line used to secure the stern of a boat or ship to a dock.

Stern wake – The trail of disturbed water left directly behind the stern of a moving vessel.

Stern wave – A continuous wave formed by the stern of a vessel moving through the water, which radiates outward from the vessel in a V-shaped pattern.

Stiffness – A sailboat's or sailing ship's resistance to heeling in a breeze and is measured by the vessel's righting moment.

Stock – The crosspiece on some kinds of anchors.

Stopper knot – a knot used at the end of a line to prevent the line from completely passing through a restricted passage such as in a block or other fitting.

Stops – See **Sail stops** and **Spinnaker stops**.

Storm jib – A small jib made of heavy or sturdy material designed for use with a reefed mainsail.

Swell – A large, long wave that travels long distances without breaking.

Tack – The direction of movement of a sailboat in relation to the side from which the wind is blowing – wind from either port (port tack) or starboard (starboard tack).

Also, the forward, lower corner of a fore-and-aft sail.

Tailwind – A wind blowing from directly astern.

Tall rig – A sailboat or ship with a tall mast or masts compared to the length of the hull. This is a subjective judgment compared to the average proportions of similar sailing vessels and has no mathematical definition.

Tether – A safety line used to connect a sailor's safety harness to a boat.

Also, a dinghy painter.

Tide – The vertical rise and fall of the ocean surface due to the gravitational attraction of the moon and sun. Tide does not refer to the flow of water, or current, caused by the tides.

Tidal current (or current) – A flow of ocean water caused by the vertical rise and fall of the tide.

Tidal current vector – A line (arrow) drawn on a chart indicating the speed and direction of the current at a particular place and time.

Tiller – A handle for steering a small boat, which is attached either directly to the rudder or to the rudder post.

Tillerman – One who steers using a tiller.

Toe rail – A low strip that runs around the edge of the deck as a foothold.

Track – The actual path of a boat through the water over the ground (sea floor) – sometimes called "ground track."

Transceiver antenna – An antenna that can both transmit and receive electromagnetic signals.

Transom – The surface that forms the stern of a boat.

Trim – The fore-and-aft manner in which a boat or ship sits in the water, either in a bow-down attitude (trimming by the bow) or a stern-down attitude (trimming by the stern). Also, the precise setting of a sail.

Trough – The valley between waves.

True north – Geodetic north, the direction along the earth's surface towards the geographic North Pole, which is located along the earth's rotational axis.

Turning block – A pulley used on a boat to change the direction of a line under tension.

Turtle – Upside down. Also, the bag used to store and deploy a spinnaker.

Underbody – That portion of a hull below the waterline.

Upwind – Same as against the wind. Upwind is not the opposite of downwind, because it is not possible to sail a boat directly into the wind.

Variation (magnetic declination) – The angle between magnetic north, as indicated by a compass needle, and true north and is expressed in the number of degrees and minutes either east or west of true north. Magnetic declination varies from place to place on the earth's surface and from year to year in any one place. See Appendix A for more detail.

Vessel – Any boat or ship.

VHF (or VHF radio) – A radio utilizing the Very High Frequency band of electromagnetic frequencies and is the principal means of line-of-sight communication between boats, ships, and shore based facilities.

Wake – The track of waves of a vessel or other object moving through the water – includes the bow wave, stern wave and stern wake.

Waterline – The line where the hull of a boat or ship meets the water's surface.

Weather – Same as windward.

Weather helm – The need to pull the tiller to weather or turn the helm to prevent a boat or ship from turning to weather (into the wind).

Weather-vane – To come around into the wind without steering assist.

Weigh anchor – To raise the anchor – to dislodge the anchor from the sea bottom and haul it aboard.

Weir – A fish trap consisting of a large net held up by a long oval-shaped cable supported by long poles driven into the ocean floor. The oval is typically about the size of a horse racetrack and has a funnel-shaped opening at one end to allow fish in but which they cannot find again to get back out.

WH a.m. – A portable Wireless Handheld Accessory Microphone used to remotely control and use a fixed location VHF radio.

Wharf – Same as a pier.

Whistle buoy – A buoy that makes a low pitched whistling sound, and sounds from a distance like the call of a dove.

Winch – A rotating drum with a ratcheting mechanism that allows the drum to rotate in one direction only and around which a sheet, halyard, or other line can be wrapped to control and secure its position. The drum may be operated with a handle attached to internal gearing for mechanical advantage.

Windward – Sailing toward the direction the wind is blowing from (against the wind).

Also, the side exposed to the wind.

Wineglass hull form – A smooth transition from the hull to an extended keel, much like the transition of a wineglass bowl to its stem, as viewed from directly forward or aft of the boat.

With the wind – Sailing with the wind blowing from any direction aft of abeam.

Working jib – The standard jib provided for a sailboat – not a special purpose jib.

Yaw – To swing about a vertical axis away from the intended heading. A sailboat tends to yaw when sailing with the wind.

ENDNOTES

1   One would think that an eastward flowing current through Butler Hole and Pollock Rip Channel toward the open sea would be associated with an ebbing current. However, Nantucket Sound fills from the south. The northward flow pushes water out toward the east through Butler Hole and Pollock Rip. When the sound empties (ebbs) to the south, the water is sucked back in toward the west through Pollock Rip and Butler Hole.

2   The "righting moment" of a boat is the torsional force that resists the tendency of the boat to heel (tip) in a breeze. The righting moment "arm" is the horizontal distance between the center of buoyancy (the central point of support exerted by the water as it pushes upward to keep the boat afloat) and the center of gravity (center of downward force or weight) of the entire boat. In the case of a deep keel craft, the boat's center of gravity is low in the keel due primarily to the heavy weight (often equal to the weight of the entire rest of the boat) at the lowest point in the keel. When the boat is at rest in the water with no wind blowing, the center of buoyancy is directly above the center of gravity and the length of the horizontal "righting moment arm" is zero. The boat is essentially "hanging" from its center of buoyancy. As the boat heels away from its vertical orientation in an increasing wind, the length of the counteracting "righting moment arm" increases as the center of gravity swings farther and farther away from its initial vertical alignment with the center of buoyancy. The boat becomes "stiffer" and increases its resistance to further heeling.

3   Okay, now you have to pay attention. As a catboat starts to heel in a breeze, the lead weights in the bilge move ever

so slightly off center. However, because the boat is shaped like a pumpkin seed (very wide and shallow), the center of buoyancy moves rapidly off center to create a long and stabilizing righting moment arm. Unfortunately, when the center of buoyancy reaches the edge of the boat and has nowhere further to go, the righting moment arm no longer increases in length and the boat's stiffness peaks. This situation occurs at a modest angle of heel. At this point the centers of gravity and buoyancy are in an almost horizontal line from each other. As the angle of heel increases further, the righting moment arm actually gets shorter because the center of gravity continues to rotate up and around toward the now fixed center of buoyancy! And the more the boat heels, the faster the moment arm gets shorter and the faster the boat becomes unstable until it feels like a Hobie catamaran up on one pontoon. Unless the skipper is good at sailing Hobies, over he (she) goes!

4   The foregoing history of Fort Jefferson was extracted from an article written by Jan Fogt who wrote for *The Stuart News* and *The Courier* in Jupiter, Florida.

5   A reliable way of setting a spinnaker so as to minimize the likelihood of fouling by wrapping itself about the forestay to form the classic hourglass shape when filled, is to first set the sail in stops before releasing it to the wind. To do this, the sail is carefully folded inward upon itself from top to bottom keeping the port and starboard edges (colored red and green respectively) running along the outside of the folded sail. As the sail is thus manipulated into a long round bundle, it is tied with "stops" made of stopping twine—sometimes called rotten twine—designed to break easily when pulled tight. The end result is a huge "rattail" that will reach from the top of the mast to the outer end of the spinnaker pole near the deck when set for deployment. When the spinnaker

sheets are pulled tight, the lower stops break apart setting off a chain reaction of breaking stops that progresses from bottom to top as the sail fills like a huge zipper unzipping. The sail then sets flawlessly—or so it says in the manual. Of course, nothing is ever always perfect.